1499

UFO CULTS
AND THE
NEW
MILLENNIUM

Other books by William M. Alnor

Heaven Can't Wait
UFOs in the New Age
Soothsayers of the Second Advent

UFO CULTS

A N D   T H E
NEW
MILLENNIUM

William M. Alnor

Baker Books

A Division of Baker Book House Co
Grand Rapids, Michigan 49516

© 1998 by William M. Alnor

Published by Baker Books
a division of Baker Book House Company
P.O. Box 6287, Grand Rapids, MI 49516-6287

Printed in the United States of America

Library of Congress Cataloging-in-Publication Data

Alnor, William M.
    UFO cults and the new millennium / William M. Alnor.
        p.   cm.
    Includes bibliographical references (p.   ).
    ISBN 0-8010-5791-4
    1. Unidentified flying object cults—Controversial literature.
I. Title.
    BL65.U54A46   1998
    001.942—dc21   98-5609

For current information about all releases from Baker Book House, visit our web site:
http://www.bakerbooks.com

To three pastors who greatly influenced me:
Joe Focht for his clarity of teaching,
Chuck Smith for his clarity in vision,
and
Oden Fong for his clarity in standing for righteousness.
They are among the real "Men in Black,"
"Protecting the earth from the scum of the universe."

CONTENTS

ACKNOWLEDGMENTS

I would like to thank many people who "stood in the gap" for me during this difficult project. Thanks to the people at Calvary Chapel who put up with my UFO talk following the Heaven's Gate disaster, and thanks go to my parents who put up with me during hibernation time.

Don Ecker of *UFO* magazine helped pull out some information on Hatonn of the Ashtar Command, and Bob Waldrep of Watchman Fellowship tipped me off to the Ancient Mystical Order of Melchizedek. Dr. Ted Daniels of the Millennium Watch Institute helped clarify some points about the Solar Temple.

I would also like to thank the folks at Baker Book House who believed in this project, notably Dan Van't Kerkhoff and Dwight Baker.

Finally, as always, thanks goes to Jackie, my wife, for helping push the project on by reading every word and serving as my first critic.

INTRODUCTION

In some ways it resembled a revival service. Framed by the sun shining in their lush yard, eucalyptus trees swaying in the background, tears often running down their cheeks, they talked, looking into the video camera, and testified of how happy they were. Thirty-eight of them—almost every member of the group—gave their testimonies during the tapings. They spoke of having no regrets about what they were about to do. They laughed and some of them cried with joy and most of them praised their leader for showing them the way to "the next level."

A short time after making the tapes, these members of the Heaven's Gate UFO cult were dead along with their leader, Marshall Applewhite. In one of the most bizarre scenes in history that was captured and transmitted throughout the world by news organizations, the thirty-nine cult members were lying on bunk beds or mattresses with their bags packed in dormitory-like rooms on a 1.6-million-dollar estate in Rancho Santa Fe, California. All but two of them were covered with a purple triangular shroud. All of them were dressed in black pants, black Nike sneakers, and a black collarless shirt with large pockets on the front.

Further astounding the world was the news that they killed themselves at the time of comet Hale-Bopp's closest approach to the earth, hoping to catch a ride in a spaceship that they believed traveled in the wake of the comet. By killing themselves, they reasoned, they were not dying. They were simply shedding earthly "containers," and this was necessary for them to enter heaven's gate.

"It's the happiest day of my life," one man said. "I've been looking forward to this for so long."

"We're very happy and proud to have been members of the Heaven's Gate group and couldn't be happier about what we're going to do," added a young woman.

"We couldn't be happier about what we're about to do," said another woman. "Doubt was never an issue."

"People who thought I completely lost my marbles, they're not right," said one person as others laughed in the background.

"We have no hesitation to leave this place, to leave the bodies that we have," Applewhite testified.[1]

When authorities arrived on the scene on March 26, a day after the last of the suicides, their bodies were rapidly decomposing. In fact the first two deputies to enter the house were sickened from the stench of rotting flesh to the point they had to be taken to a hospital to make sure they had not been poisoned by the noxious gases. Later other law officials arrived at the death scene and, donning face masks, were able to find out more. First, those dead were not all young men as initial reports suggested. Twenty-one were women and eighteen were men, with ages ranging from twenty-six to seventy-two. The mistake occurred because the cult members all had short-cropped hair and loose-fitting clothing.

The victims were also easy to identify. Almost all of them left a packed suitcase or a bag on their bed. Most had their birth certificate, their passport, and their driver's license in their pockets. Each had a five-dollar bill and some quarters alongside his or her identification. The glasses of those who wore them were folded up and tucked neatly beside their head. At first, authorities didn't know how they had died. But the suspicions of the medical examiner were confirmed by evidence found in the house. Some of the cult members had notes in their pockets that contained instructions for suicide. Also in the house in a blue spiral binder was a note titled "The Routine," which confirmed what the medical examiner already concluded, that the group died in three waves: "15 classmates need assistance." Then, "15 more need assistance." Finally, "Help each other." The last two to die were the only men not covered by the purple burial shrouds but they each had a plastic bag over their head. Authorities later found other plastic bags that were used to suffocate the cult members after they had taken poison.

The instructions had been to mix a large dose of crushed phenobarbital tablets—a strong sedative—into pudding or applesauce, then wash it down with straight 100 proof vodka. To make sure they all died, others placed a plastic bag over their head, securing it at the neck with a rubber band to ensure suffocation. It was foolproof.

Officials also confirmed that the deaths took place in three waves, with the first group of fifteen dying on March 24, a second group of fifteen dying on March 25, and a final group of nine dying on March 26. In the last wave, apparently the two men who were found uncovered helped the other seven kill themselves, then covered their bodies with shrouds before they finally succumbed themselves. The planning was meticulous.

How could something like this happen? How could these people who ran a high-tech computer business actually believe that by killing themselves they could go to a better world in "angel-like" bodies, as their leader put it? After all, by the time of the suicides, rumors of a spaceship trailing the comet were decisively debunked.

When law officials began contacting the victims' next of kin, they discovered that most of them had not been in touch with their biological family in many years. Despite the fact that they had been engaging in commerce with various companies in their computer Web page business, they were isolationists. As is the case with many communal living cults, strict limits were placed on their activities. For the most part, outside influences were shunned, and members were governed by strict, but voluntary, rules that even limited communication with other members. In many ways cult members were even told how to think. As journalists and scholars pored over their many rules and regulations, it became clear that members were taught groupthink, and that to remain in good standing, they had to unconditionally and unquestionably submit to the leadership of the cult.

As the *Philadelphia Inquirer*'s Carol Morello pointed out, cult members considered themselves actually wed to the group—they had been seen wearing identical wedding bands as they toured the country, and they were governed by three "major offenses," and an additional thirty-one "lesser offenses" that ranged from "gossip, laziness and procrastination to aggression, selfishness and vanity":

> First was deceit, defined as "doing an act 'on the sly.' Lying to my teachers or any of my classmates. Keeping an offense to myself. Not exposing it the same day."
>
> Second was sensuality, defined as "permitting arousal in thought or action (nipping it in the bud)." At least six of the 18 men, including Applewhite, had been castrated, and the group preached celibacy out of the belief that sexual deeds and reproductive organs could bar them from ascending to the "Next Level."
>
> The third major rule was an encompassing prohibition against "breaking any instruction or procedure knowingly."[2]

As this book will point out, due to the tremendous documentation they left behind in cyberspace that spans hundreds of pages, there are not many mysteries left about the cult. It turned out they had been planning their suicides for some time. The documents also confirm what I have known from studying cults for almost twenty years, that a cult can be an extremely dangerous system, both spiritually and physically, particularly when the leader of the group begins to show signs of aging or poor health. In the case of Heaven's Gate, many members thought Applewhite was dying and that after he was gone there would be nothing left for them.

Cults can become dangerous not only to society but to themselves, if they believe they are under attack. Take the People's Temple cult of the Rev. Jim Jones in the 1970s, for example. While they were settled in San Francisco, there were no calls for mass suicide. That didn't happen until after the newspapers and magazines, and later government officials, honed in on them and exposed widespread corruption and abuse in the cult. The exposés led Jones to take his people to the isolated jungle in

Guyana, where he feared attacks from the CIA and other sources. It was there in the jungle where the suicide drills began and it was also there in the isolation that Jones could almost totally control what his People's Temple members learned, saw—and eventually drank. The primary spark for the mass suicide of that group in 1978 was the visit of U.S. Congressman Leo S. Ryan, who was gunned down at an airstrip as he attempted to leave Guyana with some members of the cult. In that case Jones told the cult members they would wake up in a better place.

The point is that there are many things fundamentally wrong with what has become known as cult dynamics in the late twentieth century. Cults are totalitarian systems that are not spiritual in nature as they claim. They will not bring one closer to God. They can bring destruction and sometimes death, spawned by their leaders' delusions.

This book is written from a Christian perspective. From my understanding of the Scriptures, it is abundantly clear to me that God does not desire people—anyone, not even his most ardent worshipers—to isolate themselves from society. The true gospel of Jesus Christ is about sharing the good news with the world and with doing good works. We are not to look for a selfish escape from this world. Since God is unchanging, so must the true faith be unchanging. Despite the problems associated with Christianity—the schisms and excesses, such as the Crusades and the Inquisition—none of the human behavior that led to the dark pages in church history was even remotely sanctioned by Scripture and the founder of Christianity, Jesus Christ. It is still a fact that Christian doctrine has not changed for two thousand years.

In contrast, the doctrines of the cults are built on shifting sands, and in the case of Heaven's Gate and many other UFO cults to be discussed in this book, this can lead to bizarre behavior and unspeakable evil.

I write not to sensationalize the UFO cults, but I do write to expose them and their futile, poisonous doctrines. In the wake of the Heaven's Gate suicides, news teams everywhere went on a search for answers to how and why the tragedy happened. Because I wrote about the group that became the Heaven's Gate

15

cult in my 1992 book *UFOs in the New Age,* I have made a number of media appearances to try to explain the event. The answers to why it happened are part of the fundamental human condition—the conflict between good and evil itself. I believe it is important for people to be inoculated against religious deception, which began in the Garden of Eden and since then has destroyed many. In the final chapter of this book I will attempt to unlock the way to accomplish that inoculation.

On MSNBC's *The News with Brian Williams* the day after the suicides were discovered, Williams interviewed "Will," a former longtime member of the cult who explained that before he broke away from the group, his spiritual needs were not being met by "conventional religions," as he put it.[3] Since he was interested in UFOs, "it was just the right time and he [Applewhite] was the right man and had the right charisma and there were enough people like myself at the time who were looking for something more.

"During the eleven years that I was originally with the group, no mention of suicide was ever made, and that was not our objective," he continues. "I returned to the group a couple of years ago and spent about four or five months with them and it was at that point that there was talk of suicide and how that would probably be the final demonstration as they put it. But that was the first time I'd ever heard any mention of suicide."

Indeed, the nature of religious deception is grave. As one ex-cult member pointed out on a radio broadcast, no cult leader ever gains recruits by a straightforward appeal, such as "Hey, I am a cult leader. Come follow me and give me all your possessions and your mind as well." Deception takes root much more subtly than that. This was certainly the case with the Heaven's Gate group. The cult's incubation stage, ending in their final evil act near San Diego in March 1997, was about thirty years long.

This is a book about the preponderance of UFO groups and space-age cults as we near the end of the second millennium. Not only will it trace the rise and fall of the Heaven's Gate UFO cult, it will look at other destructive space-age groups, such as the Solar Temple and Japan's Aum Supreme Truth cult, that have

16

been in the news in recent years. It will also look at various UFO and space-related movements that have not yet received widespread attention. All of these groups are bizarre, and because they, like the Heaven's Gate cult, have irrational beliefs, this book may at times startle the reader. But it is not my intention to sensationalize this subject or astound the reader as we look at these cults. Rather, as we survey these groups, I will explain how they have formed and will try to unlock the puzzle of why so many of these groups exist today and why their number appears to be rising.

My hope, as a longtime researcher of the cults, the occult, and the paranormal, is to shatter the mystique of such cults by exposing their deceptions. I will also show that there is a frightening spiritual agenda behind groups such as the Heaven's Gate and that spiritual deception is evil as it leads to irrationality and sometimes death. It is therefore quite clear to me that other bizarre acts, like the Rancho Santa Fe suicides, could happen again as we enter the dawn of a new millennium.

RIDING ON THE TAIL OF A COMET

"Well, when I had been dead about thirty years, I began to get a little anxious," Captain Stormfield said. "Mind you, I had been whizzing through space all that time, like a comet. *Like a comet!*"

That's when Stormfield, the hero in a fictitious story, decided to race an "uncommonly big" comet "about three points off my starboard bow." As he moved closer to the huge object at hundreds of thousands of miles per hour, he noticed men riding on the comet who were up for the drag race with him. But something went wrong. Sensing the excitement, Stormfield reported that "upwards of a hundred billion passengers swarmed up from below and rushed to the side and began to bet on the race." The shift in weight caused the comet to change course, and this also got Stormfield hopelessly lost in space. Eventually, after going through a void of darkness, he approached a huge structure of blinking lights in the distance that looked "like mighty furnaces." But he realized he wasn't headed toward hell; he was drifting toward one of heaven's gates, along with millions of people from many other worlds.[1]

This strange fiction about heaven being in our own dimension somewhere out in space with the world of planets, stars, and comets was not dreamed up by UFO cults. It was actually the whimsical short story, "Extract from Captain Stormfield's Visit to Heaven," written in 1907 by Samuel Langhorne Clemens, alias Mark Twain, the most famous American author of all time. Although the story was meant to be a comedy of sorts, it did contain a strange mix of serious theological musings and speculations about heaven and who would make it. It turns out that one aspect of the heaven's gate that the fictional Captain Stormfield stumbled on was like the heaven imagined by the Heaven's Gate cultists in 1997: Only a few worthy earthlings ever made it there because planet Earth was so degenerate. It turns out that in Twain's heaven, they call Earth "the wart."[2]

In "A Curious Pleasure Excursion," Twain, tongue in cheek, also puts forward the idea of passengers riding on comets through space. This earlier story that appeared in the summer of 1874 in the *New York Herald* was meant to spoof "the comet scare" that summer, caused by an approaching comet. Twain, writing in an advertising format, announced that for two dollars the public could board the comet for an incredible ride through the cosmos. "The comet will leave New York at 10 P.M.," Twain wrote. "We shall prepare 1,000,000 state-rooms in the tail of the comet. . . . We shall have billiard-rooms, card-rooms, music-rooms, bowling-alleys and many spacious theaters and free libraries." But "no dogs will be allowed on board," he wrote, adding that passengers' safety will be attended to, as "a substantial iron railing will be put up around the comet, and no one will be allowed to go to the edge and look over unless accompanied by either my partner or myself."[3]

Over the centuries many writers like Twain have been fascinated with comets.[4] Jules Verne, in his 1877 fiction *Hector Servadac (Off on a Comet),* parodied the public's obsession with comets in his story about a collision with a comet that shattered the earth into many fragments. In the story a group of survivors stranded on a fragment drifting through space encountered "the uprooted Rock of Gibraltar floating through the void with two stiff-upper-lip Britons aboard, playing chess and pretending that nothing has happened." He followed that novel with the sequel describing another comet ride called *To the Sun.*[5]

Superstitious beliefs about comets have surfaced throughout history as new comets are seen traveling through the solar system. William Shakespeare was not alone in assuming that comets were omens. His *Julius Caesar* mirrored the prevailing wisdom of the centuries in noting that their appearance represented the death of rulers. "When beggars die, there are no comets seen," he wrote. "The heavens themselves blaze forth the death of princes."[6] This belief that comets signaled the death of leaders was well in place by the first century. Around A.D. 60 after a bright comet appeared, many assumed that it meant the end of the savage Roman emperor Nero. But Nero, who was propped up by an astrologer's reasoning, believed he could deflect the wrath of heaven by killing prominent members of his court. Not only did he do this, but he murdered his mother, two wives, most of his family, set Rome on fire, and blamed the early Christians for it. His twisted reasoning worked for a while; he survived until just after an A.D. 66 visit by Halley's comet when at age thirty-two he committed suicide.[7]

Although there is no evidence that comets portend the death of rulers, as Shakespeare wrote, this was a long-held belief that can be traced far into the ancient world. And there does appear to be an element of truth to the fact that the arrival of prominent comets has caused misguided people to do twisted things—including suicide—through the centuries. The arrival of Halley's comet in 1910 led to at least one attempted suicide and caused some strange behavior, such as people sealing their windows to avoid alleged poisons from the comet's tail. Worldwide, there were scattered reports of strange reactions to the approaching comet as a general feeling of fear set in. There were also those who parlayed this fear into hucksterism. People sold do-nothing comet pills that promised to ward off the supposed ill effects.[8] It is little wonder then that the arrival of Hale-Bopp, which was said by astronomers to be one of the brightest comets in history, is also associated with suicide.

Comets have been portents of evil in other cultures too. According to comet expert/author Nigel Calder:

21

. . . the Incas of Peru regarded comets as intimations of wrath from their Sun-god Inti, and they presumably sacrificed a few more children to calm him when Halley passed by in 1531 shortly before Francisco Pisarro conquered them. In twentieth-century Oklahoma, at the apparition of Halley in 1910, the sheriffs arrived just in time to prevent the sacrifice of a virgin by demented Americans calling themselves Sacred Followers.[9]

Today we know a lot more about comets than in Shakespeare's or Twain's time. The truth of the matter is, "the appearance of comets has nothing to do with earthly events such as the overthrow of governments or the death of world leaders. Instead, astronomers say mankind's centuries-old myths about comets work the other way around. Since there are always so many comets coming around the sun, one can always attribute a war or death to a comet."[10]

"Comets are coming in all the time," says Villanova University's astronomy professor Frank Maloney. "On the average a half dozen new ones are coming in every year. And the rate has remained unchanged in the past 120 to 130 years. They're not coming in any faster in the past several decades."[11]

But in the world of the cults and for those predisposed toward mysticism and superstition it doesn't matter what the astronomers and modern science say about comets. Cults often believe comets *are* significant; they often mean something. If they can't discern an immediate meaning, they will search for one, even if it defies logic. Thus, historically, the appearance of comets has often resulted in aberrant behavior. The cult deaths in San Diego in 1997 were not the first suicides linked to an approaching comet.

The Hale-Bopp Companion

How did the Heaven's Gate suicides happen? The cult was enthralled by rumors from amateur stargazers that several objects, "companions," were following the Hale-Bopp comet. They added two and two together and came up with five—that the "companions" traveling in the wake of the comet were UFOs. This conveniently coincided with their strong conviction held since the 1970s—that a UFO would someday appear in the sky and whisk them away. As Hale-Bopp zoomed closer to Earth and the debate over the supposed "companions" intensified, cult members refused to accept reports from scientists that the alleged objects were distant stars. They chose instead to believe that a spaceship tailed the comet. It was "a marker" signaling the end of their life on earth, and they died expecting to wake up aboard a UFO. How deceived they were!

This wasn't the first time cult craziness had been linked to an arriving comet. In 1973 the late David Berg, also known as Moses David, the far-out leader of the Children of God (COG) cult (now called The Family), used the approach of the "star grazing" comet Kohoutek to convince his nomadic cult members to flee the United States.[12] Why? Because he said the comet would bring mass destruction to America. "40 DAYS! And 'Ninevah' Shall be _DESTROYED!_" trumpeted the cult's pamphlets that were passed out across America. "Jan. 31 _THE END?_" they asked, displaying what looked like a diagram of a collision course with planet Earth.

But when Kohoutek turned out to be the dud of the century instead of the destruction of America, Berg blamed COG members and outsiders for misinterpreting the comet.[13] It was the _tale_ of the comet, not the tail of the comet that was important, he wrote. And the tale—the prophecy of judgment against the United States—was still valid, he railed.

Lest one think this cult was just plain kooky, some Christians on the fringe of the mainstream also got in on the act. In 1979 the Southwest Radio Church, which is on more than one hundred radio stations nationwide, stated that Kohoutek was the herald of U.S. President Richard Nixon's ouster and the fall of many other world leaders. "Even though Kohoutek may have been a scientific fizzle, its prophetic mission to foretell the doom of rulers was an amazing success," trumpeted writers David Webber and Noah Hutchings.[14]

Man-Made Gods of the Stars

People are capable of incredibly irrational behavior, history reveals. But still I believe that within the heart of every human being there lies a God-shaped void. I also believe that if people don't find the *right* God, there is an evil being in the world that will be more than willing to help them find the wrong one. I believe this was the case with the Heaven's Gate cult. Those who followed leader Marshall Applewhite to their death were obviously convinced that they had found a way of salvation. Instead, they found death; they were deceived.

Many have cracked jokes about the bizarre deaths. Heaven's Gate has been fodder for the late-night talk shows. Web pages poking fun at Heaven's Gate have sprung up. Of course it is wrong to laugh at even the most bizarre tragic events, but recently a member of my church handed me a newspaper cartoon dealing with the Heaven's Gate tragedy that did capture the terrifying irony of the deaths. There they were in the cartoon, the thirty-nine members of the Heaven's Gate cult, crowded in a dark cavern with the devil himself, horns, pointed tail, pitchfork, and all, standing in front of the group, a smile on his face. "Hey, where's the UFO?" a cult member asks Satan.

Whoever says that rational, intelligent people can't get caught up in intense irrational deception certainly doesn't know history. People want to believe in something larger than themselves; some are in a lifelong search for ultimate meaning as they go from fad to fad and from one pop spiritual trend to another throughout their whole life. History teaches us clearly that matters of religious faith and the belief in the supernatural are often not based on facts and rationalism. Some people are willing to believe in irrational systems—and even proven lies no matter how outlandish they may be. Thus the late twentieth century has seen a great proliferation of cults.

I do not think there is any one cause for what appears to be an explosion of cults and deception now. I believe there are many reasons, starting with the breakdown of the traditional family, that have led to the fragmentation of society. I also believe

24

that the mass media have played a role in this, both in presenting mystical ideas to a gullible public, and also in helping to fuel an intense interest in UFOs and other space-age concepts among the general population. The media have also helped to create a dependence on the media—and on high technology, which has further resulted in isolation of individuals. This has helped lead to the computer age and to cyberspace, which has helped many disappear into a fully interactional world of their own liking.

These factors have all helped to alienate many in our contemporary culture. No longer have the church and traditional societal forces set the agenda for society. No longer can governments have much of an impact on the way citizens think. People have at their fingertips a world that goes beyond boundaries.

The Heaven's Gate cult was fully wired into cyberspace and into the science fiction portions of the Hollywood entertainment industry. They were well aware of matters of astronomy, ufology, and science fiction and were occupied with building computer Web pages for their clients. But they were ignorant of the traditional things—they were aloof from their natural families, the government, and tradition itself. In the end, they even tried to look alike, convinced that killing their passions, worldly ambitions, and life's desires—being sexless, androgynous beings—was a step in the right direction, or as they put it, a step to the "next level."

Irrationality and a fascination with the stars in space similarly marked ancient religions to the point of murder. In Old Testament times many civilizations in and around Israel had child sacrifice as part of their Baal worship system, which brought the wrath of God down on the people. At about 650 B.C. the reigning king of Judah was Manasseh, who assumed the throne at age twelve. "He did much evil in the sight of the LORD," 2 Kings 21:6 states, "to provoke Him to anger." As an earlier king of Israel had done, Manasseh sacrificed his son to Molech and brought back Baal worship to Judah. He ordered idols of other gods placed throughout the land and "bowed down to all the starry hosts and worshiped them." He even built altars to the stars and planets, "practiced sorcery and divination, and consulted mediums and spiritists," the Bible states (2 Kings 21:3–6 NIV).

25

This type of sorcery—sacrificing children to the false gods of Baal—continued on and off throughout the history of ancient Israel in ways that are difficult for modern humankind to understand. In both the Books of Ezekiel and Jeremiah, the prophets noted that God was particularly angered by the practice of those who killed their children in the fire in the nearby Valley of Hinnom just outside Jerusalem, then walked to his temple to worship him.

What many don't realize, though, about these pagan sacrifice rituals, which were all linked to the murderous Baal worship system that covered the ancient world, is that they, like modern-day UFO cults, have a link with solar bodies in space. The cult god, Ashtoreth, also known in the Bible as Astoreth or Asherah, was actually the female consort of Baal, according to the pagan legends, and was one of many gods in the Canaanite pantheon, or company of gods worshiped in the Middle East.[15] According to *The Bible Knowledge Commentary,* in Syria she was known as Athtart and in Babylonia as Ishtar.[16]

Somehow Baal worship was intrinsically fused with the worship of the hosts of heaven such as the sun, stars, and planets. The Israelites, in keeping with the worship of surrounding nations, had sacred horses and ceremonial chariots that were used in formal processions honoring the sun. This was especially true of Ashtoreth, "whose worship involved licentious rites and worship of the stars."[17] According to the *New International Dictionary of the Bible,* Gesenius, the biblical scholar, "related the name Ashtoreth to the Persian word 'sitarah' or 'star' and connected it with Venus, goddess of love."[18]

Sacrificing children to Molech was also part of that cruel pagan worship system that fused astrology with fortune telling, divination, mediums, consulting with familiar spirits, witchcraft, star and idol worship, and other practices that are in vogue with modern New Age occultism. Molech, according to the *Davis Dictionary of the Bible,* was considered to be an "aspect" of Baal.[19] *Boyd's Bible Handbook* notes that the Old Testament prophet Amos likened human sacrifices to Molech to sacrifices to Chiun, or Saturn, and adds that when Stephen was about to be martyred in the first century, he named one of Israel's sins as idolatry, "mentioning 'Rephan,' which is Saturn or Chiun (Amos 5:26; Acts 7:41–43)."[20]

The purpose of this is not to become too theological. It is simply to say as the wise King Solomon said so many years ago that there is "nothing new under the sun." When one analyzes ancient religions, one cannot help but notice that the human heart hasn't changed. Many ancient cultures courted obsessions with space objects that sometimes coincided with death rituals and suicide.

And as we move toward the turn of a new millennium, the year 2000 and beyond, the world is not moving into a glorious new age as many occultists want us to believe. Rather, we are moving into a new era of deception and barbarism that in some ways is similar to the ancient pagan world. Space-age cults, like the Solar Temple, Heaven's Gate, and Aum Shinri Kyo (Supreme Truth), are leading their followers into a new dark age. People who, like sheep, blindly follow irrational leaders are often led to their ruin.

Although there are very real differences between ancient and modern cults, parallels do exist between them. Cult systems of both eras have led to death for some. For example, in the Mayan death rituals of more than a millennium ago atop pyramids in the Yucatán peninsula, sons and daughters were sacrificed to appease their astrological gods. In some of today's cult systems people have died seeking a new future in another place, whether by boarding a UFO or being reborn on another planet. The results of these beliefs in both time periods are unspeakably evil.

A Space Link to the New Age

I anticipated some of the recent tragic events four years ago in my book *UFOs in the New Age,* which warned of a growing UFO religion. To put it together, I traveled more than twenty thousand miles, attended various UFO and New Age conferences, read hundreds of books, and interviewed many experts on UFOs. I talked with many contactees and abductees (people

27

who claim they are regularly contacted and sometimes taken against their will by aliens from outer space) and even attended several sessions during which aliens were allegedly giving messages to crowds. I concluded that the UFO "movement" around the globe has blossomed into a power religion akin and actually part of New Age occultism. It has an apocalyptic bent as well. Its goal, generally speaking, is to change the world. It wants us to reject traditional Judeo-Christian ideas about God, morality, and even reality itself in favor of a new world order and an occult-based spirituality.

According to *The Fellowship,* a book by New Age occultist Brad Steiger that contains messages from around the world delivered by the so-called space brothers, this is how the alleged aliens hope to help earthlings in the dawn of a new millennium:

> Contactees have been told that the Space Beings hope to guide Earth to a period of great unification, when all races will shun discriminatory separations and all of humankind will recognize its responsibility to every other life form existing on the planet. The Space Beings also seek to bring about a single, solidified government, which will conduct itself of spiritual principles and permit all of its citizens to grow constructively in love.[21]

The UFO Cults

As the Heaven's Gate suicide cult has shown us, there are UFO cults out there that don't want to bring a new world order to this planet. They want to escape this world instead. There are many UFO believers scattered around the world who believe, just as the Heaven's Gate cultists believed, that the space brothers are coming on an evacuation mission for a small number of worthy earthlings. As the theory goes, these worthy earthlings will be redeposited back on planet Earth to help rebuild it after a series of cataclysmic changes and even a polar shift. This *is* far-fetched, yet there are many UFO enthusiasts worldwide who intensely believe this will soon happen. In fact such beliefs are not out of the mainstream of ufology!

Knowing this and having documented it in my previous book, I was not the least bit surprised when thirty-nine members of the Heaven's Gate UFO cult committed mass suicide in late March 1997. My background in researching religious cults has shown me how erratic they can be. As this book will show, similar events involving other UFO cults may happen in the future.

The Solar Temple cult is another suicide cult that has some similarities to the Heaven's Gate cult. Since 1994 seventy-four members of the Solar Temple cult have either killed themselves or been murdered in various waves in Switzerland, Canada, and France. The leader, Joseph Di Mambro, who died in the Switzerland suicides in 1994, held bizarre beliefs that were linked to outer space. In addition to his claim that he had been a member of the Knights Templar during the Crusades in a previous life, he told his followers that after their fiery deaths, they would magically wake up on a planet called Sirius.

Some space-age cults have minor similarities to the ill-fated Waco, Texas, Branch Davidian cult in that they talk frequently about the Book of Revelation and of a fiery battle of Armageddon as leader David Koresh did. But unlike Koresh, they believe their salvation will come from flying saucers either before or after their apocalyptic scenarios of the future.

Some destructive cults have small doses of space-age science fiction theology woven into their doctrine. One such group that has come to light in recent years is the powerful Aum Shinri Kyo doomsday cult of Japan. This is the group, headed by Shoko Asahara (who claims to be Christ), that is accused of killing twelve people and injuring 5,500 in a sarin nerve gas attack in a Tokyo subway station on March 20, 1995. According to the cult's theology, the gas attack was a step in hurrying along Armageddon, an ensuing great struggle, which would eventually lead to a new world order. Missing in many law enforcement accounts of the cult's activities, however, are explanations as to why Asahara thought it would work. *Why would he want to kill people?* It turns out that Asahara was deeply influenced by discussions of intergalactic conflict and war in some of the science fiction of Isaac Asimov! In fact he modeled his sect after characters in Asimov's most famous science fiction novels.

Intergalactic wars and space fantasies are also the stuff of the Church of Scientology, which many agree (along with *Time* magazine) is a worldwide sinister cult of greed. It was founded in the 1950s by the late L. Ron Hubbard, a science fiction writer.

Other prominent cults, such as the Nation of Islam, headed by Louis Farrakhan, have more hidden theories of UFOs and mass destruction. According to published reports, Nation of Islam members were attracted to the *Independence Day* movie of 1996 because it portrayed massive spaceships in the same manner that Farrakhan said would come. Although the fiery leader wasn't likely to espouse such views at high-visibility events such as the Million Man March on Washington, D.C., in the mid–1990s, his belief in huge, destructive UFOs is well known. According to the September 18, 1995, *Washington Post,* Farrakhan claims to have been taken aboard a UFO more than thirty years ago, after which he was taken to a larger "mother ship." While there he talked with "Master Elijah Muhammed," the builder of the ship, who was still alive.

Unholy Religious Promotion

The bottom line is that many bizarre UFO cults that have not based their faith on facts or even reason have the potential to be just as lethal to their followers (and potentially to others) as the Heaven's Gate was. The devotees of these groups appear to be following pied pipers off the dock and into the swirling water.

Many adherents of the most bizarre groups are bright enough to be on-line into the complex world of computers and cyberspace. Just as the Heaven's Gate cult did, they have complex Internet Web pages on which they display their fantasies for the entire world to see. Sometimes they entice new believers to join them. The Internet is a new—and easy—way of recruiting potential followers and it has created a new set of problems for cult watchers. The Internet has made bizarre ideas available to the entire world, almost instantaneously with just the click of a computer mouse and Internet browsing software. Although the Internet is a marvelous communication and research tool, its peculiar nature works both ways, in that it allows for reckless and sometimes dangerous ideas to be absorbed quickly by gullible people. Prior to the Internet there were more built-in curbs on ideas. Editors of newspapers and magazines served as gatekeepers, individuals with the power to ignore or discredit wacky ideas instead of publishing them. The Internet has allowed anyone with know-how and a standard modern computer equipped with a modem to go on-line to receive and disseminate ideas worldwide, without being curbed or censored by an editor.

Here is a summary of some of the activities of other UFO cults in the wake of the Heaven's Gate disaster. I will deal with each of these in more detail in this book.

- A French UFO cult, lubricated with a great deal of money and a rabid worldwide following, is pursuing technology with the goal of cloning human beings. This same UFO leader has announced plans to build an embassy in Jerusalem to welcome the space brothers and to build Disneyland-like UFO theme parks in Canada and near Orlando, Florida. He already claims to have been whisked away on a spaceship to heaven, which he says is actually an alien planet.

- For decades a San Diego UFO cult has been maintaining landing pads near the city for the return of the space brothers and dozens of flying saucers. The cult's leaders declare that the flying saucers will arrive and usher in a new era in 2001.

- A woman, who claims she is really an angel from the stars, has convinced thousands of people throughout the world that they are about to be "ascended" to the next level to join their brothers and sisters in the stars. Will she do something to further push them along? Does she really believe her own claims or is she, like so many others within the New Age movement, a charlatan seeking money and recognition from her vast number of followers?

- One UFO cult, claiming that the new age began on January 23, 1997, is making pilgrimages to what the cult claims are "nine holy mountains" worldwide. They claim that a New Age Christ from another world has arrived. This group is one of several popular New Age cults making the same claim that they say comes from the so-called space brothers.

- Another belief system that is found throughout ufology is the legend of thousands of spaceships and angel-like creatures commanded by a supernatural spaceman known as Ashtar. The ships circling Earth are ready to beam people up in preparation for the coming new age. Believers in this will also be happy to show drawings of numerous aliens waiting in their spaceships. Just a click on a computer mouse will get you to their Web page.

The Hollywood-Alien Affair

Since *UFOs in the New Age,* UFO cults have become even more high-tech—and more bizarre—and the public's fascination with UFOs, aliens/angels, and the paranormal has continued to grow. Some of this, undoubtedly, has been sparked by television, which produces shows like *Dark Skies, Sightings,* and *X-Files.* In addition, the Hollywood film industry creates films about aliens, such as the 1996 blockbuster *Independence Day* and one of the summer of 1997's biggest hits, *Men in Black.* Filmmakers know that space lore and science fiction themes sell, and in both *Independence Day* and *Men in Black,* filmmakers have successfully exploited certain UFO legends for the silver screen, literally bringing folklore to life. In the comical *Men in Black,* filmmakers gave a story line to the popular 1950s idea that in the wake of UFO sightings, men dressed in black clothing, the "UFO silencers," would visit the homes of people who had claimed a UFO sighting or contact, and harass them into recanting their stories. The men in black of Sony's film are in reality secret government agents involved in clandestine battles with aliens, some of whom have been attempting to become naturalized U.S. citizens. They are "protecting the earth from the scum of the universe," taunt the movie promo spots.

"On the basis of box-office draw, three science fiction or fantasy features led the all-time list of American movies," wrote media history professor Michael Emery, before the 1997 release of *Titanic* topped them all.[22] According to Movieweb, an Internet site, six of the eight top-grossing movies of all time contained science fiction or space themes. The top eight are: *Star Wars* (1977 and 1997, $460 million), *E.T.* (1982, $407 million), *Jurassic Park* (1993, $357 million), *Forrest Gump* (1994, $327 million), *The Lion King* (1994, $313 million), *Return of the Jedi* (1983 and 1997, $307 million), *Independence Day* (1996, $306 million), and *The Empire Strikes Back* (1980 and 1997, $290 million).[23]

Films and tales of alien landings and tagging along with a comet are all in the realm of fantasy. There are no facts to support the bizarre beliefs of the end-of-the-millennium space cults. This is in stark contrast with Christianity, a faith based on history and founded on fact. Jesus did not just claim to ascend to his Father in heaven following his crucifixion; eyewitnesses saw him do it. And there were more than five hundred eyewitnesses who saw him after his resurrection. Not only was his resurrection recorded in the Bible, but various Roman writers discussed it as well.[24]

Christianity stands alone today as a bulwark in a time of what may be unprecedented religious deception and fables. Unlike the beliefs of UFO cults, belief in Jesus the Messiah operates in the realm of reason and in the clear light, not out of the realm of shadows, secrecy, and alleged alien visitors, abductions, and contactee messages that can be extracted only by hypnosis. Christianity stands against the hostility and distortion of the UFO cults.

A Telepathic Hoax

The seeds of destruction were always there for what became the Heaven's Gate UFO cult.

After germinating for almost twenty years, it all began to come to a head in 1993 when the cult, which had gone underground due to bad publicity many years before, decided to resurface with a vengeance. And they increasingly began to go on-line through the Internet to proclaim their message of doom—and UFO salvation—to the world.

They began slowly that year with an ad campaign and on May 27 the cult, which had previously been known by various names, including The Two, the Bo and Peep UFO cult, and HIM (standing for Human Individual Metamorphosis), published a one-third-page statement in *USA Today* that announced to the world not only that the cult was back, but that the world was going to be "spaded under."

"The Earth's present 'civilization' is about to be recycled— 'spaded under,'" the statement trumpeted. "Its inhabitants are refusing to evolve. The 'weeds' have taken over the garden and disturbed its usefulness beyond repair." Between June and September of that year the cult, which was now operating under several other names, among them Total Overcomers Anonymous (TOA), placed similar ads in over twenty weekly and monthly alternative newspapers and magazines in the United States, Australia, and Canada.

And in 1994 they began to spread out, leafleting the country and proclaiming their grim message of a coming judgment. Teams went to many states that year as the cult attempted to reestablish itself as a major player, proclaiming to all who would listen salvation through the coming UFOs but also spreading a message of judgment. They produced posters and distributed them nationwide. On one, dated November 28, 1993, they claimed to possess "THE ONLY WAY OUT OF THIS CORRUPT WORLD." The poster offered "membership in the *true* Kingdom of God" and proclaimed that human physical bodies are only *"containers"* for souls.

Throughout 1994 their messages seemed to grow grimmer—and more desperate. They began to offer themselves as the "last chance to advance beyond human."[1] A poster that Heaven's Gate produced, dated March 16, 1994, stated, "'UFO CULT' RESURFACES WITH A FINAL OFFER." It went on to say that a physical kingdom level *"cannot* be entered 'after you die.'" Instead this kingdom "exists in the literal heavens, with its own unique biological 'containers' or bodies, and modes of travel—spacecrafts or 'UFOs.'" "'Leave All Behind' and Go with Them—or Take Your Chances," proclaims another poster, dated June 20, 1994.

So by the time 1996 rolled around, the die was cast—and much of the escape plan was placed on their Internet Web site and on videotape. By September 1996 Marshall Applewhite, who had called himself Do, was announcing a "last chance to **evacuate Earth** before it is **recycled.**"[2] A few months later Applewhite (who had declared himself an incarnation of Jesus Christ) was talking about his own death and that he would have to lay down his own body. Meanwhile, Heaven's Gate documents indicated that other cult members were thinking of their own death as well. They began recording detailed "exit statements," which did not talk of suicide outright, but rather of shedding their containers and moving to the next level.

36

In a January 1997 statement posted to the World Wide Web and to ninety-five specific news groups on the Internet, Applewhite also declared that the cofounder of the group, Bonnie L. Trusdale Nettles (alias Te, who died of liver cancer in 1985), was God the Father. The statement said, among other things:

> I am about to return to my Father's Kingdom. This "return" requires that I prepare to lay down my borrowed human body in order to take up, or reenter, my body (biological) belonging to the Kingdom of God (as I did approximately 2,000 years ago, as Jesus, when I laid down the human body that was about 33 years old in order to reenter my body belonging to the Kingdom of Heaven).[3]

From that point on, it seems, all of the members of the Heaven's Gate cult stepped up their efforts to join a UFO. They were preparing to die.

Comet Hale-Bopp was an excuse, but it wasn't as simplistic as news reports made it out to be. There were definite reasons cult members believed a UFO was trailing Hale-Bopp.

What they didn't know was that part of their reasoning was based on one of the biggest hoaxes of the century, launched in part by an amateur astronomer and a late-night talk show host and ignited by an occult-oriented political science professor from Emory University, who had long been obsessed with channeling and wild stories of Martians, galactic federations, and extraterrestrials (ETs).

Art Bell Coast-to-Coast

Broadcasting daily through the early-morning hours from his modular home in the tiny desert town of Pahrump, Nevada, Art Bell has become something of a national cult figure in UFO circles. Bell broadcasts for five hours, from 11 P.M. to 4 A.M. Pacific time, and more than ten million night owls tune him in on more than 340 radio stations in the United States and Canada. He has two shows, *Coast to Coast AM* on weeknights and *Dreamland,* a three-hour show on Sunday evenings that begins at 7 P.M. Pacific time. His shows often focus on the, uh, weird. Want to hear the latest about the Bermuda Triangle? Bigfoot? alien abductions? pyschic surgery? government conspiracies? the Abominable Snowman? Martians? Then Art Bell's shows are for you.

Photographic Deception

It turns out that the rumor got started on Bell's show that at least one UFO was following the Hale-Bopp comet. It began on the November 14, 1996, show when amateur astronomer Chuck Shramek of Houston photographed comet Hale-Bopp and thought he saw a mysterious "Saturn-like object," as he put it, trailing it. Within hours his observations lightninged through the Internet World Wide Web, and later that night Art Bell put Shramek on his *Coast to Coast* broadcast to announce his discovery. In announcing the find, which later turned out to be a distant star that was partly distorted by the spewing tail of the comet, Shramek said he didn't know what it was but that he hoped other astronomers would look for it.

Astronomers looked and announced that the object was a star. But prior to their announcing their findings, an occult-obsessed professor, Dr. Courtney Brown, of Emory University, who had just listened to the Shramek interview, immediately called in and came on the air during that same broadcast to explain what Shramek had seen. It was a UFO hauling aliens to our vicinity, said Brown. And how did he know? Because he had focused his mind on it and that's what he saw via "remote viewing." Remote viewing is a form of spiritism or channeling that Brown regularly practiced and had previously discussed when on Bell's show as a guest. It was a "monstrously large hollow planetoid filled with aliens . . . heading toward Earth," and we would "meet them SOON," he declared.[4]

Area 51

It is little wonder that one of Art Bell's shows in which he regularly examines UFOs and other paranormal subjects is called

Dreamland. This is the title ufologists have given to an infamous site located about three hours to the north of Pahrump that has long been linked to alleged UFO landings. It was at this site, popularly known as Area 51, or the Groom Lake U.S. government base, where the decisive battle against enemy aliens was fought and won by downloading a computer virus into the aliens' mother ship in the blockbuster movie hit of 1996, *Independence Day.* That movie portrayed one of the most persistent UFO legends about Groom Lake within ufology: that the U.S. government may be hiding there at least one alien ship (which presumably crashed near Roswell, New Mexico, in 1947, another famous UFO legend) and possibly the bodies of aliens who died in the alleged crash. Although this and many other unsubstantiated rumors abound, some of them being incredibly outlandish, most skeptics and the U.S. government discount them.[5] For example, most UFO experts have resoundingly debunked the so-called "alien autopsy" film released to a fascinated public in 1995 as a hoax.

However, hoaxing aside, there is little doubt that the Groom Lake U.S. government base is a testing ground for the next generation of top secret aircraft and spy planes. It is common knowledge, now, that various top secret, high-tech craft were largely developed at the site, including the U-2 spy plane. According to an Area 51 Internet Web site, Area 51 was "selected in the mid–1950s for testing of the U-2 spy plane, due to its remoteness, proximity to existing facilities and presence of a dry lake bed for landings." It continues: "Groom Lake is America's traditional testing ground for 'black budget' aircraft before they are publicly acknowledged."[6] What does the government say about the base today? Almost nothing. Those who try to penetrate the base by land or air are aggressively shooed away.

The Evolving Legend

Getting back to the story of how the UFO-following–Hale-Bopp hoax developed, shortly after Courtney Brown's declaration that the object was an alien ship, another remote viewer, Ed Dames, came on Art Bell's show to give more credence to the idea that something big was about to happen with the so-called companion object. And Dames, a former associate of Brown, added a terrifying twist to the evolving legend. The companion was a "hollow metal cylindrical object," but it was *not* boarded by aliens. It was a bomb of sorts. It would "rain death and destruction via disease upon the earth, wiping out 85 percent of the world's population, and this was supposed to happen SOON."[7]

Best-selling horror and UFO writer and alleged alien contactee Whitley Strieber also came on the Art Bell show to give credence to the companion theory. On the broadcast that followed soon after the initial report of the companion object, he suggested that listeners meditate on the object because the "visitors seem responsive to this." (According to Strieber, the visitors, as outlined in three of his books, *Communion, Transformation,* and *Breakthrough,* are ufonauts who have possessed his body and chosen him as their agent to help bring in a new age to the planet.[8])

The public loved the idea that a UFO was trailing Hale-Bopp, and more rumors about the comet abounded. People were downloading photographs onto the Internet, displaying alleged "eyes" trailing the comet, while others were claiming that Hale-Bopp had changed its course, which indicated it was acting on its own accord, even being directed by ET intelligences.

Members of the Heaven's Gate cult were apparently listening to the companion stories, and were eating them up. They obviously put a lot of stock in Bell's broadcasts. Not only did the Heaven's Gate Web site contain a link to Bell's site, they referenced Bell's show in one of many Internet Usenet postings. And in a posting to a newsgroup dealing with the Church of Scientology in December (alt.religion.scientology), a Heaven's Gate representative cited Bell's broadcast as offering "fantastic proof that the 'Next Level' mothership is coming."

But even by the time of that posting, the alleged Hale-Bopp companion had been exposed on Bell's show and in numerous other media outlets as a hoax. One of those who helped expose it (on Bell's program and through interviews with reporters) was Alan Hale, the New Mexico astronomer who had, along with amateur astronomer Thomas Bopp, discovered the comet on July 23, 1995. "This whole thing is nutty," Hale told the *Albuquerque Journal,* explaining that the images were stars in the background.[9]

But Hale's pronouncements, which echoed those from NASA and almost every astronomer in the world, were not heeded by many UFO buffs. Hale and others were engaged in a huge government conspiracy to keep the public from the truth and the alleged conspirators felt the wrath from radical ufologists. Hale was flamed as "an Earth traitor" by an Internet critic after he helped debunk the companion theory.[10] The *Albuquerque Journal* also quoted a NASA scientist who discredited the theory, along with Harvard astronomer Daniel Green:

> "What's upsetting is that they won't take the time to learn" [Green said in discussing the companion theory and the subsequent wrath some were receiving for disagreeing with it]. . . . "If there was a mysterious object flying alongside the comet," said Green, "amateur and professional astronomers around the world watching the comet would have seen and reported it.
>
> "That's the way science works. That's the way astronomy works. You can't hide anything," said Green, who works for the International Astronomical Union, an international clearing house for such information.[11]

The bottom line is that even after the story had been debunked—even on Bell's show—the Heaven's Gate cult still apparently believed the story and were saying so in more muted terms by the time they took their own lives in late March. They were planning to kill themselves anyway, and Hale-Bopp was the "marker" they proclaimed on their home page:

> Whether Hale-Bopp has a "companion" or not is irrelevant from our perspective. However, its arrival is joyously very significant to us at "Heaven's Gate." The joy is that our Older Member in the Evolutionary Level Beyond Human (the "Kingdom of Heaven") has made it clear to us that Hale-Bopp's approach is the "marker" we've been waiting for—the time for the arrival of the spacecraft from the Level Beyond Human to take us home to

"Their World"—in the literal Heavens. Our 22 years of classroom here on planet Earth is finally coming to conclusion—"graduation" from the Human Evolutionary Level. We are happily prepared to leave "this world" and go with Ti's crew.[12]

And so they left this world in a bizarre suicide ritual, leaving the world horrified. Chuck Shramek, the one who discovered the so-called "Saturn-like object" trailing Hale-Bopp, was one of those horrified. But he wouldn't take responsibility for the suicides. "Of course I am upset and saddened by the cult suicide but in no way do I feel I caused this tragedy," he declared in a March 28, 1997, press release that called Applewhite an "apparent madman." He placed much of the blame on Courtney Brown and a few others. He said:

> Immediately after having me on the air, Art [Bell] then had Professor Courtney Brown of Emory University in Atlanta on as a guest. Courtney professes to be able to teach people "psychic remote viewing," an alleged way to view events at a distance using psychic powers. Courtney then proceeded to go into great detail in describing the odd thing near the comet as a giant spaceship, filled with aliens. For several hours Courtney Brown then talked about the strange ship near the comet. Other guests on the Art Bell show also agreed with Courtney that a spaceship was near the comet. One guest who identified himself as a former NASA worker even said the craft was filled with creatures who were part human and part dolphin! I want to make it clear that I am not the source of the spaceship stories regarding the comet.[13]

Remote Viewers Discredited

Eventually, according to *Time* magazine, it was Art Bell and others who discredited Courtney Brown after Brown claimed he had proof in the form of a "photograph of the craft taken by a 'Top-10-university astronomy professor,' who had told him radio signals were coming from the object, indicating it was 'intelligently driven.'"[14] "That revelation, Bell reported on his elaborate and well-attended Web site, 'practically blew away my disbelieving side.'" Bell placed the photograph on his Web site, demanding proof of its authenticity, and within twenty-four hours the photograph was shown to be a fake. Under fire Brown never declared the origin of the photograph, nor would he give the identity of the alleged Top-10 professor. "It's important to understand that the only person who ever said there was a spacecraft following Hale-Bopp was Courtney Brown," Bell told *Time*.[15]

Another controversy that fed into the Hale-Bopp rumor mill that caused some to believe the comet was something more than typical was the fact that as the comet closed in on the inner planets, it did slightly change its course. This news was transmitted on the World Wide Web as more proof that the comet was somehow being guided by an intelligence. Once again, the truth came forward but it didn't end the fictitious comet speculations. Edwin Kripp, the director of Griffith Observatory in Los Angeles, said that Hale-Bopp's change of course was normal because it neared Jupiter; all comets that pass that close to Jupiter are pushed into new orbits by the giant planet's gravity.[16]

Bell then had Ed Dames on the show to let Brown have it. It was Dames who had agreed with Brown that there was a companion object trailing Hale-Bopp. Dames thought it was like a bomb. Dames said he could not accept Brown's views of the object because Brown did not comply with his techniques of remote viewing, which Dames said were "100 percent accurate."[17]

A bit later Bell challenged the credibility of Dames. On the March 25, 1997, broadcast Bell had three of Dames's former associates on the air who declared that "Dames has created more than one fabrication about his own history and that he had been preaching one sort of doom or another for years." Indeed, on Dames's computer bulletin board, members had been discussing clearing their bank accounts and moving around the world to escape the impending doom.[18]

It turns out that Dames, a former army major, has also remotely viewed alleged aliens and has been quietly spreading his teachings. According to the June and July 1993 *New Mexico Mutual UFO Network News,* Dames claimed that he was shown, via remote viewing, that there would be an alien landing in New

Mexico "before the end of August" 1993. It would be a "vanguard colony" of about thirty aliens, perhaps from Mars, he declared. He added more details of his visions:

> Apparently some 150 million years ago the Martians were living comfortably on Mars. A large celestial object of some sort sideswiped the planet and sucked away part or all of the atmosphere. The Martians must have foreseen this disaster because they built shelters (pyramids), stocked them and moved in. . . .
> The Martians, apparently hoping that the planet would regenerate its atmosphere over time, remained in their pyramid/hibernation chambers. They ate all the food and began to die; the population dwindled to 15 percent.[19]

Some of these Martians, he later related, were rescued by other space aliens from "the Federation," representing, like *Star Trek*'s Federation of Planets, a dozen or so different interstellar traveling races. They are being transported to planet Earth where they are involved in genetic hybrid experiments with humans, Dames declared. Some, however, are enchambered still on Mars:

> . . . others are in a "goop" that sustains them and into which their wastes filter. Some of the Martians are upset about the gooped ones because they have been in the goop so long (150 million years?) that they've totally changed in the horrid conditions and can now only communicate telepathically. One can imagine; the remote viewers did not enjoy seeing this, it made some of them physically sick.[20]

Brown Rewrites the Bible

Courtney Brown also talks extensively about the Martians and about another race of alleged aliens called "the greys," an idea that is heavily debated in UFO circles. In his book *Cosmic Voyage*[21] Brown says that Martians were brought here by "the Greys" (described in popular UFO literature as short, grey creatures with praying mantis–shaped heads and huge black eyes), who have helped "relocate them in several Earth locations, including in caverns underneath Santa Fe Baldy, just north of Santa Fe, N.M."[22] He claims the Martians, who look very much like humans, will soon make contact with the United Nations. Furthermore, he writes, the "Greys are building a new Earth-like planet where some humans will be relocated as our environmental trouble rapidly accelerates in about another 50 years."[23]

Some of Brown's other remote viewings are just as far out. Not content to just discuss aliens and outer space theories, Brown also delves into matters of the Christian faith. In fact it might be astounding to some that he teaches political science at Emory University, a United Methodist–related college, while practicing occultism and denying the very principles of the Christian faith!

The news of Brown's entanglement in the UFO hoax reached Emory, of course, and there have already been calls from other faculty members to fire him. But Emory President William Chace at press time was holding firm on not seeking Brown's dismissal on the basis of academic freedom and also because Brown's remote viewing theories were related to Brown's independent Farsight Institute, which has "no relationship whatever with Emory University." "While I do not agree with the content of Professor Brown's non-Emory activities, he has the right to pursue them," Chace concluded in his statement to the press.

The photograph that turned out to be a hoax and Brown's activities with the Farsight Institute could be grounds for his dismissal from Emory. His practice of remote viewing is an occult technique akin to trance channeling. Remote viewers claim that by concentrating and focusing their mental energies on objects, they can perceive information at great distances across space and time. Psychics who are sometimes called in during bizarre cases use remote viewing to focus in on killers and circumstances in unsolved murders and mysteries. Apparently the U.S. government (and other governments, including that of the former Soviet Union) has experimented with remote viewing applications for intelligence purposes. Allegedly, remote viewers were utilized during the Gulf War to attempt to find Saddam Hussein's chemical and biological weapons.

But what should rankle evangelical Christians and particularly cult watchers is the occult means and training Brown utilizes in his remote viewing activities. In his 1996 book, *Cosmic Voyage,* he suggests learning advanced transcendental meditation (TM) as remote viewing training.TM, among other things, is an Eastern religious cult practice, not a recognized scientific technique as many of its practitioners claim. It was introduced into Western culture by Maharishi Mahesh Yogi and is steeped in belief in gods and demigods.

In addition, Brown steers people to Robert Monroe and the Monroe Institute in Faber, Virginia. As I wrote in my book *Heaven Can't Wait,* Monroe specializes in out-of-body experiences and "bizarre elements of occultism and necromancy"—specifically forbidden in Scripture.[24] In his book *Journeys Out of the Body* Monroe claims to have had numerous paranormal experiences with dead persons, including "out-of-the-body trysts and disembodied sexual encounters."[25] Tal Brooke, president of the Spiritual Counterfeits Project of Berkeley, which is one of the most outstanding evangelical Christian ministries that oppose cults, said that prior to his conversion he was involved with Monroe while an undergraduate at the University of Virginia in the late 1960s. He writes in *The Other Side of Death* that Monroe was conducting experiments at that time to induce astral experiences.[26]

It should be pointed out that Courtney Brown is not the only Ph.D. who teaches at a respected university under the glare of negative publicity for views on aliens, abductions, and even alien harvesting and hybrid experiments on humans. Dr. John Mack, a Pulitzer prize–winning Harvard professor and psychiatrist, wrote *Abduction* in 1994 that alleged that aliens abduct people. Some wanted him removed from Harvard. And there is also Temple University's David Jacobs, who espoused similar views in his books *Secret Life* (1992) and *The Threat* (1998). He, likewise, has suffered criticism from some quarters of that university.

What has Brown been shown via remote viewing that contradicts the Bible, and therefore Christianity? First, he says, Adam and Eve were *not* placed in the Garden of Eden as the Bible states. He saw them via remote viewing and they were not "naked primitives in a lush garden," he said. They were aliens— "genetic engineers who were responsible for seeding the planet with a new species that evolved into humans."[27]

Brown also claims a different view of God than Christianity and Judaism teach. He teaches a New Age god, not unlike that proclaimed by Shirley MacLaine, animists, shamans, and New Age channelers. Their belief is that God is part of nature. "It seems that God is sentient and literally exists in fragmented form in evolving life and everything else," Brown said. "It is as if God experiences joy in creating matter and life from his own substance and then living life through the experiences of species everywhere."[28] This, of course, is in contrast to the God of the Bible who is distinct from his creation. Solomon declared that "the heavens, even the highest heavens, cannot contain him" (2 Chron. 2:6 NIV). "In the beginning God created the heavens and the earth" (Gen. 1:1).

Brown also makes serious errors about the person of Christ, who the Bible declares is God in human flesh, the second person of the Holy Trinity. Brown places Jesus on a par with Buddha and other religious leaders. But the Bible declares that Jesus is the only way to God the Father (John 14:6). The apostle Peter, filled with the Holy Spirit, declared to the Sanhedrin just weeks after they had ordered Jesus' crucifixion that "God raised [Christ] from the dead. . . . This is the 'stone which was rejected by you builders, which has become the chief cornerstone.' Nor is there salvation in any other, for there is no other name under heaven given among men by which we must be saved" (Acts 4:10–12). To those biblical declarations, Brown would dissent. His source? Remote viewing. He says that he concentrated on Jesus one day and wound up contacting him via remote viewing.

"He was wearing a gown, and he was somewhat translucent," Brown told the *Fort Worth Star-Telegram*. "His hair seemed to be made of light. I soon got the impression that Jesus wasn't this austere fellow I grew up believing he was. He seemed quite friendly, and I detected a sense of humor." The article then went on to quote Brown as saying that Jesus taught the theory of evolution:

Jesus' message wasn't all that different from that of 2,000 years ago: All things are a manifestation of God's love, and no life form is more important than another. The only difference between bees and bears, humans and extraterrestrials is their degree of evolution. Humans, Jesus told Brown, must help others in their evolutionary path. This includes extraterrestrials.

"Jesus didn't just say we should work with them," Brown said. "He conveyed the clearest concept of a command that I have ever received from any being while remote viewing."[29]

But through remote viewing, Brown said, Jesus did appear to get angry when he asked him if "non-Christians had to call on him to evolve fully." To that, Brown said, Jesus said no. "Quite forcefully, he stated that a name is nothing. Everything depends on personality development. Understanding and loving God is the important thing. That is what carries us through evolution."[30]

The reason I am presenting Brown's statements as they relate to biblical Christianity is to explain that there is a basic incompatibility between the two. The real Jesus of the Bible did not teach what Brown's revelations say he taught. Jesus taught that he was the only way of salvation. He said, "I, if I am lifted up from the earth, will draw all peoples to Myself" (John 12:32). The Bible teaches that Jesus came to give his life as "a ransom for many" (Matt. 20:28)—to die for the sins of the world, past, present, and future. "For by Him [Jesus] all things were created that are in heaven and that are on earth, visible and invisible, whether thrones or dominions or principalities or powers," the Bible declares in Colossians 1:16. "All things were created through Him and for Him." And it is he, the passage continues, that is holding the entire universe and its myriad of worlds and stars together: "And He is before all things, and in Him all things consist" (Col. 1:17).

It is apparent that Brown is giving us a perverted gospel and a different Jesus than the one proclaimed in God's Word. Paul warned the Galatian church that there are some "who trouble you and want to pervert the gospel of Christ. But even if we, or an angel from heaven, preach any other gospel to you than what we have preached to you, let him be accursed" (Gal. 1:7–8).

The Secret to Remote Viewing

As we have seen in examining some of their outrageous claims, the Hale-Bopp remote viewers cannot be trusted. As Hale-Bopp zooms to the outer reaches of the solar system, not due to arrive again for another 3,400-plus years, it is obvious there was no companion object chasing it as Brown claimed, nor was there a death bomb on it as Dames said on national radio.

Today's remote viewers have received their information in the same unreliable way in which Erich von Daniken allegedly received his inspiration for his discredited best-selling "ancient astronaut" books—through spiritism. These books (among them were *Chariots of the Gods?*, *Gold of the Gods*, *Return to the Stars*) contain faked photographs, hoaxes, and/or misleading artifacts and embellishments in von Daniken's attempt to prove that ancient astronauts actually seeded planet Earth with humans. Further, he alleged, many of the biblical stories are made up and show alien intervention in human history. The ancient ark of the covenant, for example, von Daniken wrote, was a radio transmitter, and Ezekiel's vision of the four flying creatures was actually of a flying saucer.

But von Daniken, as Timothy Ferris reported in articles he wrote in 1974 and 1975 in *Playboy* and *Rolling Stone,* prior to his adventures into the archaeological arena, had multiple fraud and embezzlement convictions in Swiss courts. During one of the proceedings a court-appointed psychiatrist pronounced him a "pathological liar" and a psychopath.[31] The *Playboy* article added that he spent a year in prison for these crimes, which included forgery, and that when von Daniken was nineteen and a school dropout, another psychiatrist said that he displayed a "tendency to lie."[32]

Where did von Daniken get his theories? The same types of places Courtney Brown got his—through remote viewing, from extraterrestrial beings, through telepathy from an unknown source, and from out-of-body travels. In fact Brown has made statements strikingly similar to those made by von Daniken in a 1974 interview when asked how he came up with his theories.

"I know that astronauts visited the earth in ancient time," von Daniken declared. "I was there when the astronauts arrived. Why should anybody believe I am able to leave my body whenever I desire and observe the past, present and future—all at the same time? Nonetheless, it is true. It has been true for many years."[33]

This type of occultism, of course, is well known in the Bible. It calls it spiritism, witchcraft, and sorcery and completely condemns it. I believe this is the same type of sorcery used today in UFO circles. I also believe it is demonic and designed to bring death and destruction to people in the same way spiritism from Courtney Brown weighed in as a major factor in thirty-nine deaths at Rancho Santa Fe in March 1997.

DEEPER INTO MADNESS

One school of thought that seems to have a lot of evidence on its side is that Marshall Applewhite and Bonnie Trusdale Nettles, the founders of the cult that became Heaven's Gate, were just plain crazy. In fact Applewhite was a patient in a mental ward when he met Nettles. He was a patient struggling with homosexuality during a descent into depression and madness, and she was the nurse who comforted him.

Prior to their meeting, however, both came from ordinary backgrounds. Applewhite was born in the small Texas town of Spur, near the panhandle. He was the son of a Presbyterian minister and attended high school in Corpus Christi, "attended a theological seminary in Richmond, Virginia, and studied music at the University of Colorado, where he had starring roles in campus productions of *Oklahoma!* and *South Pacific,*" according to the *Philadelphia Inquirer.* The newspaper continued:

> He married and took his wife to New York where he tried to pursue a singing career. But the couple, who had two children, broke

51

up after he didn't land any major roles, one of his professors recalled.

... Applewhite returned to Texas, and, in 1966, began teaching music at the University of St. Thomas, a small Catholic college in Houston. He became involved with the Houston Grand Opera, singing 10 roles in productions there. The *Houston Chronicle* reported ... that Applewhite was fired from the college for "health problems of an emotional nature."[1]

According to published reports, Applewhite's repeated problems with homosexuality drove him to depression. According to Hoffman and Burke's *Heaven's Gate: Cult Suicide in San Diego,* he had earlier been fired from his job as a music professor at the University of Alabama at Tuscaloosa in the 1960s. "The reason? Administrators learned he was involved in a steamy homosexual relationship with a student."[2] His firing from the Houston college occurred under very similar conditions. At that point, Applewhite checked into a psychiatric hospital, seeking a cure for his homosexual desires.[3] That is when he met Bonnie Trusdale Nettles, the woman he claimed would rescue him and open a whole new world to him.

According to *Heaven's Gate: Cult Suicide in San Diego,* where much of the following biographical material comes from, "Applewhite was fast losing his mind, hearing voices, and battling with the demons of his confused sexuality—and Nettles was the angel in white who rescued him."[4] They talked for hours in the hospital, and shortly after he left, Nettles left her husband and grown children to take up with Applewhite, convinced that they had known each other in a previous life.

When Applewhite and Nettles founded their UFO cult in 1974, cult members were unaware of their connection to the mental ward. In fact Applewhite and Nettles lied about the circumstances surrounding their meeting. In later literature from the group there was an attempt to gloss over the fact that they had met in a mental institution. One statement reads that Applewhite met her while he was visiting someone in a hospital.

Nettles and Applewhite Jump into the Occult Together

Louise "Bonnie" Trusdale Nettles was born in 1928 and was raised a Baptist. She was "trained as a professional nurse, married, and raised four children in near obscurity in the Houston area." However, her life "slowly, inexorably began to change in the turbulent '60s." Hoffman and Burke write: "Like many in those years of the so-called Age of Aquarius, Nettles cultivated an intense, almost religious interest in reincarnation, astrology, and mysticism. Unlike most others, she never abandoned it."[5]

Nettles then left her family to open with Applewhite the Christian Arts Center in the First Unitarian Universalist Church in Houston, where they openly practiced astrology. In 1974 they claimed they were "awakened" to the knowledge that they were aliens sent to Earth to collect converts for a ride back to the stars. The Two, as they were also known, also dabbled in Theosophy in the formative years of their building a following. Although they later denounced these teachings, it is significant that they were heavily influenced by them.

Put simply, in many ways Theosophy was the predecessor of what was to sweep the world in the late twentieth century under the umbrella designation the New Age movement. The Theosophical Society was founded by spiritist Helena Petrovna Blavatsky in 1876, and later broke off into "four prongs" during the twentieth century, and "each 'prong' has made a significant impact on current New Age Christology," according to Dr. Ron Rhodes, a Christian author and apologist.[6]

Although Blavatsky, who was born in Russia and later lived in Philadelphia and New York, was an alleged drug addict and was exposed as a fraud for weaving various tall tales on her way to forming her own religious movement, she still amassed a worldwide following. Her two chief works, *Isis Unveiled* and *The Secret Doctrine*, which reportedly plagiarized at least two other books, are still widely used by Theosophists today.[7]

What makes this link interesting is that "Blavatsky claimed to have received numerous messages from spirit beings—aliens—as early as the 1880s. New Age occult writer Brad Steiger wrote that Blavatsky's beings were

> part of a governing hierarchy between man and the solar rulers of the universe. It is said that the mighty beings who would later become Earth's adepts came from Venus six and one-half million years ago. Venus is said to be the original home of the Lord of this World, the Head of the Hierarchy of Masters, and the Three Lords of the Flame.[8]

Bo and Peep on the Road

After Applewhite and Nettles met and imagined a mystical connection with each other, they began developing their ideas about UFOs in an attempt to build a large following, sometimes by holding public meetings. But then trouble came. Applewhite was arrested and convicted on a car theft charge and spent four months in jail. Heaven's Gate literature dealing with the conviction generally agrees with other accounts of what happened. Applewhite and Nettles had resorted to living on credit cards while building their following. At one point Applewhite rented a car and did not return it. Both were arrested on charges related to credit card theft, and Applewhite was sentenced to four months in a St. Louis jail.

The jail time did not dissuade the couple, however. Following Applewhite's release, the couple took their show on the road, visiting cities throughout the United States trying to build a following of people who wanted to be taken aboard UFOs and brought to the next level. It was also during this time that the two began to think of themselves as Jesus and God the Father.

They crisscrossed America proclaiming their message, though generally concentrating on the western states. Their message was simple: They wanted to gather a select group of people worthy enough to be taken aboard UFOs and ushered off to a new place. Everyone who wanted to go had to leave everything—and everyone—behind, and join them on a flight to the stars where they would be "above Human." The reaction to their message was sensational, as the media began to pick up the bizarre story. It also had a touch of mystery attached to it as wives began to leave husbands and children began to leave parents. The cult was spawning a growing army of dissenters.

In Oregon in 1975 the cult burst onto the national consciousness. "A score of persons from a small Oregon town have disappeared," CBS's Walter Cronkite calmly informed the nation on October 8. "It's a mystery whether they've been taken on a so-called trip to eternity . . . or simply been taken." They had simply joined the cult and many later returned home.

Bad publicity followed their catapulting onto the national scene. Bo and Peep, as the pair were often called, faced ridicule from near and far over their outlandish claims that saucers were about to land and whisk away their followers. They were asked to prove themselves to the world with some miracles. They'd do better, they said. They'd give the world a sign. Since they were the two witnesses in the biblical Book of Revelation, they were going to be slain in some large American city. Three and one-half days later they would rise from the dead and leave Earth aboard a UFO![9]

What they were referring to, of course, is in the eleventh chapter of Revelation. Describing what many Bible scholars say will be an incredible future event, it reads:

> I will give power to my two witnesses, and they will prophesy one thousand two hundred and sixty days, clothed in sackcloth. . . . And if anyone wants to harm them, fire proceeds from their mouth and devours their enemies. And if anyone wants to harm them, he must be killed in this manner. . . . When they finish their testimony, the beast that ascends out of the bottomless pit will make war against them, overcome them, and kill them. And their dead bodies will lie in the street of the great city. . . . Then those from the peoples, tribes, tongues, and nations will see their dead bodies three and a half days, and not allow their dead bodies to be put into graves. . . . Now after the three and a half days the breath of life from God entered them, and they stood on their feet, and great fear fell on those who saw them.
>
> Revelation 11:3, 5, 7–9, 11

They even picked the city—Oakland, California—and time they would be assassinated and summoned more than one hundred of their followers from Oklahoma and St. Louis to witness it. But they left their followers "wandering aimlessly along the California coast for about a week" when they became "no shows" for the event.[10] Despite their repeated declarations that it was about to happen, it never did, and Bo and Peep, or The Two, who also called themselves Te and Do, had a lot of explaining to do. When their predictions didn't happen, there were many defections from the cult. Among the high-profile departures in April 1975 was that of Joan Culpepper, whose Southern California home was the birthplace of the cult, which was then known as Human Individual Metamorphosis (HIM).

"We want to let the people know the trip has changed," Culpepper told the *Sacramento Bee*. ". . . Bo and Peep are no longer planning on an assassination and resurrection."

Later in the *Sacramento Bee* interview Culpepper, in explaining how she was setting up a shelter for others who wanted to defect from the UFO cult, claimed that the cult exercised frightening mind control over its followers. "We plan to take care of our own and believe me, they need it," Culpepper said. "Their brains are scrambled. It took me two months, two months, to get back to reality."[11]

But if Culpepper was stunned that the cult had not delivered on its promises, she wouldn't have been if she had known the background of Nettles and Applewhite. The assassination theory was one of many promises they did not keep as the cult progressed. But even before its birth, their lives were based on lies and deceit.

Years later, in the cult's 1988 statement, they were still trying to explain away what went wrong in 1975. Like most cults do when prophecy fails, they spiritualized the prophecy, stripping it of a literal meaning. They said that Applewhite and Nettles *were* killed during the ordeal—by the media. This is reminiscent of what happened when Jesus failed to return in 1914 as the Jehovah's Witnesses proclaimed to the world. When that didn't happen, the Jehovah's Witnesses eventually began claiming, just as it does to this day, that Jesus *did* return. However, he returned invisibly, the Jehovah's Witnesses believe.

The 1988 Heaven's Gate statement explains it like this:

> Te and Do felt that the demonstration was still the one thing that could change that [public ridicule]. However, they grieved literally for days, feeling like they had been shot down by the media and the mission was dead.
>
> They received instruction to not walk into a physical demonstration but rather to know that the "killing in the street" of the two witnesses had occurred at the hands of the media. However, they felt like this was a cop-out or a "chickening out" interpretation of the one act that was the basis of their whole following. So with much embarrassment, they called their students together, convinced that without a physical demonstration their students would have every right to call them charlatans. Much to their surprise the students, almost without exception, accepted the interpretation and said, "O.K. then, where do we go from here?"[12]

That wasn't the only false statement the group received in 1975—its first year. Repeatedly Applewhite and Nettles, traveling from place to place throughout America, promised that the UFOs would pick up their followers and zoom them to another level *later that year.* They said it would happen in Waldport, Oregon, where they recruited twenty to thirty townsfolk.[13] Then they claimed the UFO would pick them up in Colorado.[14]

There were also legal problems for the duo. The two had been arrested in Texas for using the name of a local television reporter to rent a hotel room for a news conference. They had been arrested in a car with stolen California license plates. This was when the police found that Applewhite was wanted in St. Louis for failing to return a rental car. At the same time, former followers of the pair complained that they had been bilked out of thousands of dollars for "educational" training by Applewhite and Nettles.[15]

Culpepper even filed a complaint against the two, alleging that she had been fleeced of "$433 for the price of a spaceship ride she never got to take."[16] No charges were ever filed.

My purpose in airing this laundry list of false prophecies and legal troubles the two got into during 1975 is to show that these events should have marked them as false prophets. But instead, after these revelations came out very publicly and they failed to fulfill the requirements of the two witnesses of Revelation (i.e., to call fire down from heaven, to stop rainfall, to turn water to blood, and to strike the earth with plagues, as in Revelation 11:5–6), *their following continued.* Their reputations, however, were greatly damaged, which was an apparent reason for their decision to take their followers underground, away from the glare of the media. And so from 1975 to 1993—eighteen years—little was known about the cult. Published reports say they camped at different sites throughout America for a while and the two continued to work with their following that had shrunk to fewer than fifty people. In 1988 they sent a rambling report to various scholars and friends. But to most people they had just disappeared. In fact in my 1992 book, *UFOs in the New Age,* I wrote that they had faded into obscurity. This was tragic for the many families who had loved ones in the cult. It was as though they had vanished, almost without a trace. All who joined the cult forsook all their loved ones and their former lives and disappeared. This is not surprising when looking at the group. Perhaps its members were following the example of The Two, Applewhite and Nettles. They were still able to amass a following of lonely souls who were eager to believe their message. As the cult evolved, they began teaching strident doctrines against human sexuality and marriage.

When Is a Prophet a Prophet?

Of paramount importance here is the issue of who would speak on behalf of God as The Two claimed to do. Even in the 1970s—before Applewhite began claiming he was Jesus Christ and declaring that Nettles was God the Father—they upheld themselves as prophets, claiming the additional role of the two witnesses in Revelation. The trouble is, when their prophecies failed, everyone should have realized they were false prophets.

When biblical prophets told of the future they were without error, and their words were usually specific—such as that Christ would be born in Bethlehem (Micah 5:2) and that he would ride into Jerusalem on a donkey (Zech. 9:9). It is simply not true, as some teach today, that modern prophets can sometimes be wrong. The Bible's criteria for prophecy is clear. According to Deuteronomy 18:21–22, we are to judge prophets on the basis of their accuracy. In Old Testament times false prophets that led people astray to follow other gods were to be judged very severely. Deuteronomy 13:1–11 metes out the death penalty to them. One wonders what would have happened to Applewhite and Nettles three thousand years ago if they were speaking amiss in ancient Israel.

Applewhite's deception continued to the very end. According to ex-members, and verified by farewell messages from several of the thirty-nine who killed themselves, Applewhite told them that he had liver cancer and had only six months to live. However, doctors performing the autopsy say there was no sign of cancer and in fact his body appeared to be reasonably healthy.

Of course one of the biggest deceptions that Applewhite dangled in front of his followers, even as the Hale-Bopp comet approached, was that they might *not* have to kill themselves to get to the next level. He told them that they might be bodily beamed up to the spaceship in a manner not unlike that of *Star Trek.* Apparently this changed. Just two months before the macabre suicide pact, a Heaven's Gate statement on their Web site, titled "Undercover 'Jesus' Surfaces before Departure," announced:

As we prepare to "lay down" our human bodies, while declaring that entry into the Kingdom Above Human is available, there may be many humans who have been recipients of "souls" in "deposits" who may exercise their free will and separate from everything of their world in order to go with us. . . . If my Father does not require this "disposition" of us [laying down their bodies]—*He will take us up into His "cloud of light" (spacecraft) before such "laying down of bodies" need occur* (emphasis mine).

I personally believe that Applewhite and many of the Heaven's Gate members were inspired by unspeakable evil. The devil's main goal on this earth is to send everyone away from God to an eternity apart from Christ. The apostle Peter wrote that the devil "walks about like a roaring lion, seeking whom he may devour. Resist him . . ." (1 Peter 5:8–9).

The Cult Reemerges

In 1993 the cult that had lived in obscurity for eighteen years reemerged with a vengeance by taking out aggressive advertising once again in *USA Today* and proclaiming that the spaceships were coming to take people away to the "level above human." They also began to appear on the World Wide Web—in cyberspace. It turns out that somewhere along the way, according to published reports, the group received an infusion of about three hundred thousand dollars from a member's inheritance. This windfall allowed them to give up the nomadic life for the indoors—and for computers. In 1995 the group bought a forty-acre compound fifty-five miles southwest of Albuquerque, New Mexico, and began to build a complex that resembled a flying saucer, made of old tires filled with concrete. According to published reports, twenty-five members worked the land, and five or six members commuted approximately ten miles to rented offices in Mountainair, New Mexico, where they conducted their Web page design business. They rented an office under the name "Computer Nomads."[17]

However, in a move not entirely clear to most observers, they left for Rancho Santa Fe in April 1996.

The cult was always so secretive that little word had leaked out to friends or even family members about its activities. So when Nettles died sometime in 1985, her children didn't hear about it until much later. The cult explained Nettles's death in its 1988 update statement. This was tucked in the middle of the document:

> Some 3½ years ago from the time of this writing, Te left her human vehicle. To all human appearances it was due to a form of liver

cancer. We could say that because of the stress, due to the gap between her Next Level mind and the vehicle's genetic capacity, that the cancer symptom caused the vehicle to break down and stop functioning. However, it was strange that she experienced no symptoms prior to the week she left her vehicle, and for the most part her vehicle slept through the transition. We're not exactly sure how many days it might have taken her to return to the Next Level vehicle she left behind prior to this task.

But death was inconsequential, according to cult members. She was still guiding the group through her contacts with Bo. In other words, Applewhite claimed to have telepathic contact with Nettles and he confirmed to his followers that she encouraged them to commit the final act. It was quite clear from reading the deceased members' exit statements that they saw her death as outgrowing her "human container," and that she, as God the Father, would continue to guide the group through a chain of command that went through Applewhite to the Heaven's Gate members.

The Cult's Beliefs

First and perhaps foremost, the Heaven's Gate cult rejected Christianity and seemed to have a profound dislike—even hatred—for orthodox Christian doctrine. They often shrouded their beliefs in Christian jargon, while calling professing Christians "antichrist."

Although they talked about salvation via an approaching UFO in which they would be transformed into angel-like creatures in a new body, their basic way of salvation was legalistic. It was based on rules and regulations, including prohibitions against marriage and anything deemed worldly. Ironically, the apostle Paul said that in the "latter times"

some will depart from the faith, giving heed to deceiving spirits and doctrines of demons, speaking lies in hypocrisy, having their own conscience seared with a hot iron, *forbidding to marry,* and commanding to abstain from foods which God created to be received with thanksgiving by those who believe and know the truth.

1 Timothy 4:1–3 (emphasis mine)

Salvation

Applewhite taught his followers that their salvation via a UFO to the Level Beyond Human could only come if they practiced self-denial and self-discipline and followed the rigid set of rules that he taught. This is why during their underground period they called themselves Total Overcomers Anonymous. They were supposed to overcome all worldliness, in preparation to becoming something beyond human. They were expected to be celibate, live in poverty, renounce family (and all outsiders), and reject any other belief system, especially Christianity. They must, according to a transcript of Applewhite's dated October 6, 1996, and appearing on their Web site:

> overcome human flesh—the genetic vibrations, the lust of the flesh, the desire to reproduce, the desire to cling to offspring, or spouse, or parents, or house, or money, or fame, or job, or, or— that could go on and on—overcoming the human flesh and its desires—even its religious desires.

Heaven's Gate also had an unorthodox view of the human soul, seeing it as separate from the human body. According to a variety of Heaven's Gate literature, the soul was a "deposit" made into bodies, or a "plant." The bodies were "containers" that allowed the evolution of the soul to the Level Beyond Human. According to *A Christian Analysis of Heaven's Gate* produced by Watchman Fellowship, there was a dichotomy of sorts to the soul:

> . . . in Heaven's Gate theology, the members of the group actually suffered two savage deaths—the first when the previous personality was destroyed by the implantation of the soul, and the

62

second when the soul abandoned the body for transport to the Evolutionary Level Beyond Human.[18]

Applewhite taught that the historic Jesus was a vehicle used for the soul's job of helping the evolutionary development of other souls locked in human bodies. This Jesus of Nazareth was not the son of God in the flesh, Applewhite taught, contradicting orthodox Christianity. Instead, he was filled with his new soul at his baptism by John the Baptist in the Jordan River, and later his soul flowed into his container in the twentieth century. This clearly contradicts the Bible, which states that Jesus was divine from the moment of conception (Luke 1:35).

Angels and Demons

Heaven's Gate also had an unbiblical view of angels and demons. They taught that angels are asexual extraterrestrial beings that host the highly evolved souls in the Evolutionary Kingdom Beyond Human. In fact Heaven's Gate taught that when they woke up in that kingdom, they would be evolved into these angelic beings. They even included pictures on their Web page of how they might look. The artist's rendition resembled a smiling alien that looked strikingly similar to Hollywood's portrayals of good aliens or how alleged contactees or abductees say they look. The Bible, however, teaches that humans will not be angels in heaven.[19] Heaven's Gate also claimed that fallen angels, or demons, resemble the aliens that popular culture depicts performing cattle mutilations or grotesque experiments on humans.

Applewhite's heaven, which was the Level Beyond Human aboard UFOs, also contrasted sharply with Scripture. His view of God was unorthodox and confusing. Although Applewhite talked about Nettles, or "Te," being his "father," there was no single God the Father in his view. According to the Heaven's Gate's January 16, 1994, document "Last Chance to Advance Beyond Human," each soul has a corresponding "Older Member" that has the responsibility of advancing its growth. This soul is their "father."

The Second Coming

Like all other UFO cults, Heaven's Gate developed a false view of the second coming of Christ. The Bible teaches throughout its pages that Jesus Christ of Nazareth will come back physically to planet Earth. There will still be nail prints on his hands when he returns. "Behold, He is coming with clouds, and every eye will see Him, and they also who pierced Him. And all the tribes of the earth will mourn because of Him," Revelation 1:7 states.

The Bible says that when Jesus ascended back to heaven from the Mount of Olives just outside Jerusalem, angels in white appeared and made it very clear how he would return—the same way they saw him go. "Men of Galilee, why do you stand gazing up into heaven? This same Jesus, who was taken up from you into heaven, will so come in like manner as you saw Him go into heaven" (Acts 1:11).

Although there is vigorous debate as to how and when it will happen, Scripture teaches that at some time in the future some believers will be caught up to heaven without experiencing death. Paul talked to the Thessalonian church about it saying we should comfort each other with this truth:

> For if we believe that Jesus died and rose again, even so God will bring with Him those who sleep in Jesus. For this we say to you by the word of the Lord, that we who are alive and remain until the coming of the Lord will by no means precede those who are asleep. For the Lord Himself will descend from heaven with a shout, with the voice of an archangel, and with the trumpet of God. And the dead in Christ will rise first. Then we who are alive and remain shall be caught up together with them in the clouds to meet the Lord in the air. And thus we shall always be with the Lord. Therefore comfort one another with these words.
>
> 1 Thessalonians 4:14–18

The cult, however, taught that the second coming occurred in 1975 and 1976 when Applewhite and Nettles received their filling as the Father and Son, and the "raptures," the lifting out of the world, were their suicides, according to Heaven's Gate's poster called "Organized Religion (Especially Christian) Has Become the Primary Pulpit for Misinformation and the 'GREAT COVER-UP.'"

In a slam directly against Christianity, the poster declared orthodox Christians as "Luciferians":

> The Luciferians, who have taken over the religions, would have their "faithful" die and go to their "heaven" without doing any of the necessary *overcoming*, for "He did it all"—"He shed His blood"—in order that you might "be saved." **You *can't* simply be a good "Christian," die, and go to the *true* Kingdom of Heaven. You can only become a *new creature, a Heavenly creature*, while a Member of the Kingdom Level Above Human incarnate in the human kingdom to take you through that "*birthing*."**

The Great Earthquake

This issue of how one can go to heaven was certainly complicated to Marshall Applewhite and the Heaven's Gate people. It is also confusing to many in general, including some who come from Christian backgrounds, from fundamentalism to the mainline denominations, from Pentecostalism to Roman Catholicism and extending to every Christian tradition, including Coptic and Greek Orthodox. Indeed, there is great confusion today throughout the world as to how one can be saved and go to heaven. But it shouldn't be complicated or confusing. An illustration from the Bible that teaches on the topic makes it clear.

Almost two thousand years ago in Philippi, near the Aegean Sea, the apostle Paul and his partner, Silas, were arrested for proclaiming the gospel of Jesus Christ. They were thrown into a dungeon and were singing hymns to God while other prisoners listened.

> Suddenly there was a great earthquake, so that the foundations of the prison were shaken; and immediately all the doors were opened and everyone's chains were loosed. And the keeper of the prison, awaking from sleep and seeing the prison doors open,

supposing the prisoners had fled, drew his sword and was about to kill himself. But Paul called with a loud voice, saying, "Do yourself no harm, for we are all here." Then he called for a light, ran in, and fell down trembling before Paul and Silas. And he brought them out and said, "Sirs, what must I do to be saved?" So they said, "Believe on the Lord Jesus Christ, and you will be saved, you and your household."

Acts 16:26–31

Salvation really does come by believing in Jesus' sacrificial death on the cross for the sins of the world. That's it. Nothing more and nothing less. Those like the Heaven's Gate cult that add things to the simplicity of the gospel are gravely and tragically mistaken (Gal. 1:6–9).[20]

Endtime Delusions

There's something about the end of a millennium that drives some people batty.

"Intense excitement prevailed throughout a large part of Europe," one scholar wrote describing the atmosphere of the dawn of A.D. 1000. They believed that Christ would return at the end of the "first thousand years of the Christian era. . . . Multitudes sold their estates to unbelievers and gave away the proceeds in charities, business was neglected, the fields were left uncultivated, and for some years the wildest confusion and terror reigned."[1]

So it is little wonder that today as we approach the end of the second millennium, we have an increase of confusion. As I noted in my 1989 book, *Soothsayers of the Second Advent,* many people (among them pop Bible scholars) have been reckless during the past three decades in a search for the "signs of the times" leading to Christ's return. They have set dates for the return of Christ, engaged in unwarranted speculation about the identity of the Antichrist, and gleaned eternal meaning from

67

many obscure newspaper clippings. Among the more outrageous rumors: Supermarket bar codes are a sign of the Antichrist; the killer bees beginning to stream into the southern United States could be the locusts referred to in Revelation 9; the four digits added to the postal zip code could be part of the endtime puzzle.

Some pop Bible scholars have concluded that Christ must return around the year A.D. 2000 because of their understanding of 2 Peter 3:8 that reads: "But, beloved, do not forget this one thing, that with the Lord one day is as a thousand years, and a thousand years as one day." According to their reasoning, this means the Lord's days are one thousand years in duration. Since they believe Adam was formed in the Garden of Eden at about 4004 B.C.,[2] then the Lord is scheduled to return in this era, which is about six thousand years later. They reason that since Genesis declares that God made the world in six days and rested on the seventh, then the order of his creation will follow the same pattern. He is now due to bring the world to a close and rest on the seventh day (or one-thousand-year time period), which they argue is the millennial time period referred to in the Bible.

But this reasoning is fallacious. It places God in a box of human reasoning. It also misreads 2 Peter 3:8, which "simply shows that God is not limited by our ideas of time."[3]

But the Bible *is* clear about *legitimate* signs of the times leading to his coming. Among them are an increase in religious deception, earthquakes, multinational wars, rampant immorality, famines, and the restoration of Israel as a nation just before the return of Christ. This happened in 1948.

Heaven's Gate was at the extreme end of religious deception. Its delusion was that Earth is going to be spaded under and that it was time to leave with Applewhite, the incarnated Jesus. It is also true that similar deceptions about the end of the world and/or the collapse of the old era and the dawning of a new age are prevalent with many cults—especially with UFO cults. Many UFO cults are also talking about the arrival of the spaceships either to help clean up the mess humankind has made of the planet or, as the Heaven's Gate cult believed, to whisk a percentage of the population away from the mess. Some UFO cults echo the Heaven's Gate belief that some day, many years into the future, the spaceships may bring them back to a Garden of Eden–like restored Earth, and they will help rebuild the planet.

Some UFO cults teach that the saucers will come following a great "cleansing" of Earth that will include islands vanishing into the sea and even a polar shift, meaning the North and South Poles will no longer be at their present locations. Whitley Strieber says in his best-selling book *Communion,* which was a major force in synthesizing the flying saucer movement that had a New Age/Shirley MacLaine–type mindset in the late 1980s, that after "the visitors" abducted him and took him aboard their craft, they showed him visions of the earth being blown to bits. Although Strieber never was sure who the visitors were, they were somehow related to UFOs, he wrote, and they chose him to spread the word about a new world religion of "communion" and eventually "transformation" with the visitors.

The Great Cleansing

Indeed, many UFO enthusiasts believe that something big and perhaps even destructive is soon coming to this planet. UFO and occult writer Brad Steiger says that during the past thirty years aliens, which he also calls "paraphysical, multidimensional gods," have been:

> accelerating their interaction with us in preparation for a fast approaching time of transition and transformation. This period, we have been told, will be a difficult one; and for generations our prophets and revelators have been referring to it as The Great Cleansing, Judgment Day, Armageddon. But we have been promised that, after a season of cataclysmic changes on the Earth plane, a New Age consciousness will suffuse the planet. It is to this end that the gods have been utilizing the UFO as a transformative symbol.[4]

This line of thinking, the idea that a cataclysmic time of destruction is coming to Earth, has continued to develop within the New

Age–UFO movement at least since the mid–1970s. Another way of putting it comes from Marianne Francis of Oregon, who started studying the occult and flying saucers at age sixteen. During the past decade she has become an important figure for the space brothers and the New Age. She changed her name to Aleuti Francesca and became founder and director of the Solar Light Retreat. She claims to have communicated with space beings from other worlds, including Venus, since 1954.[5] They tell her, she says, that earthlings should not be afraid of the difficult times coming to the planet, because it means things are changing for the better.

In a channeling "transmission" from the alleged space brothers titled "Cleansing Must Come to Planet Earth," she said there is nothing to fear if people go along with the new program that includes a brand-new way of thinking by individuals and mass "changes of consciousness" that will enable humankind to embrace a new "Age of Light unto the New dimension and the New consciousness which is the Christ consciousness."[6] But for those caught holding on to the old ways of thinking, well, they may just disappear from the face of the earth.

"Prepare yourselves," the extraterrestrial messengers told her, "for the day now closely approaches and those who are not so prepared must vanish from the face of this your Earth. . . . Those who align themselves with the things of the Old must surely be destroyed with that age of decay and darkness."[7]

Influential New Age leader/author David Spangler, who headed the education department at the Findhorn Community (New Age) in Scotland in the early 1970s, says that he has had many conversations via channeling with angels and other entities, including space beings. In his 1976 book, *Links with Space,* Spangler wrote that an entity named John, who is a "spokesman for a group of intelligences on the inner places of Being," told him that humankind is teetering on the brink of destruction and may have to build an ark like Noah did to save themselves.[8] "You are building the ark [by developing a new mass consciousness associated with the new age]. . . . All who attune to and live this consciousness are absolutely protected, no matter what happens in the outer world."[9]

Some UFO cults, such as the Mark-Age Metacenter of California, which claims to receive messages from a variety of space people on a regular basis, believe that a great spiritual ruler, who has been called by different names (including Jesus and Buddha) in previous lives, is coming back to Earth, following a "cleansing period, the purification time." This Mark-Age group, one of the older UFO cults, has previously been linked to the death of a woman who was allegedly dispatched to Washington, D.C., in 1962 by an alien to convince the U.S. government to stop its warlike ways. Her name was Gloria Lee, and according to published reports an alien called J.W., transmitting spiritual messages to her, ordered her into a fast to purify her for the task. She fasted for sixty-six days, slipped into a coma, and died.[10]

Some UFO cults use biblical imagery to describe this coming time of troubles or the landing of the space brothers to usher in a new age. Steiger explains that after the space brothers come and usher in the new golden era, the planet will become "Christed," meaning that peace, goodwill, and prosperity will finally envelop the planet. Other UFO enthusiasts say this coming period will be the age of the "Holy Spirit." Some refer to the time of troubles coming as the "Tribulation" and even as "Armageddon," both of which are mentioned in the Bible's Book of Revelation.

UFO Evacuation or Salvation

Many New Age groups, including some that do not have UFOs as a central plank in their belief system, have also been thinking about the apocalypse. During the past decade some have been accused of stockpiling weapons. This was an aspect of the Heaven's Gate story that was not picked up by the media. The cult was living with a siege mentality of sorts to the extent that they had been stockpiling weapons. According to Heaven's Gate writings, if something like the government sieges at Ruby Ridge and the Branch Davidian compound near Waco,

Texas, should happen to them, they would have to defend themselves.[11]

Some other cults accused of stockpiling weapons during the past decade have been the Church Universal and Triumphant (CUT) in Montana, the Aum Supreme Truth group in Japan, and the Solar Temple group that has been linked to more than seventy deaths since 1994. In CUT's case, leader Elizabeth Claire Prophet, claiming to be "the light of Christ" (in addition to her being one of the two witnesses in the Book of Revelation), prophesied in the late 1980s that the United States and Russia would fight a nuclear war in 1990. In anticipation, the cult built bomb shelters and stockpiled weapons and as the time approached more than two thousand followers journeyed to the sect's complex/headquarters in Montana near Yellowstone National Park.[12]

But not all New Age–UFO cults talking about the apocalypse think about it in the same way. A close examination of their literature reveals that there are two basic modes of thought concerning the future. The first line of thinking is the one the Heaven's Gate cult followed: *a UFO evacuation.* This is the idea that the flying saucers are coming to evacuate the worthy people from a dying earth and to usher them to heaven or to a better planet. It may be possible, it is believed, for those evacuated to someday return to help rebuild the earth.

The second belief is the opposite: *a UFO salvation of planet Earth.* This line of thinking states that the earth is progressing forward through evolution to the dawning of a new age. If people are not spiritually in tune with the coming changes to the planet or if they resist the coming of the new era, they will be removed from Earth. Some scenarios have these people simply vanishing supernaturally, or at least their influence will be diminished on Earth because they refuse to change. Others believe UFOs may come and remove these wrong thinkers from Earth. The bottom line in this school of thought is that teams of space brothers will land throughout the planet to help humankind build a new society in tune with a great galactic federation.

Of the two lines of thought it is hard to say which is more prominent. However, the second was given an added boost by the Fox Broadcasting Network's weekly show *The Visitor* that made its debut in September 1997. The series portrays the adventures of a messianic figure sent to Earth by aliens in a spaceship to help guide the planet at this perilous time in its history. In the first episode the visitor, who was formerly a pilot lost in the Bermuda Triangle, propounds the theology of the Far Eastern gurus and makes his escape from hostile U.S. government hunters by resurrecting from the dead!

Some UFO groups, such as the Guardian Action International organization, which has been operating in the American west, in Utah, Colorado, and New Mexico, channel the so-called Ashtar Command. Ashtar, an information source popular with New Age–UFO enthusiasts, is supposedly the supreme commander of a fleet of spaceships circling the earth that are here to help guide humankind into a new age. One of the Guardian Action International's most popular books, supposedly channeled by the Ashtar Command, is called *Project: World Evacuation.* It has on its cover a colorful picture of flying saucers hovering over a city and beaming dozens of people up into the ships. In this 1982 book, with a foreword purportedly written by Jesus Christ, the Ashtar Command warns that a "great separation" is coming. It says that a "cleansing action" is coming and that people will be removed from Earth in three waves, "Exodus I, II, and III."[13]

Similarly, in another story from the early 1980s, Gabriel Green of Yucca Valley, California, who founded the Amalgamated Flying Saucer Club, one of the largest UFO groups in America at the time, was quoted by United Press International as saying that when Armageddon comes, so will the aliens "swooping down in spaceships to evacuate one-tenth of the population in what Christians call 'the rapture.'"[14]

Different Ashtars

All this can get confusing due to the many different voices in ufology giving us alternative visions of the apocalypse. Much of the information coming to UFO enthusiasts today comes through occult channeling, and it is contradictory. For example, while the

Guardian Action League has told its followers that there will be three waves of mass evacuation onto starships, there are various messages from the Ashtar Command on the World Wide Web released through Spiritweb that say something quite different. Spiritweb is a Web site run by one of the most influential coalitions of New Agers. According to some of their messages, allegedly from the Ashtar Command, there won't be any evacuation. Instead, Ashtar Command will help guide Earth to a new age of love and peace. This will happen through a massive spiritual "ascension" of humankind. It will not be a physical ascension onto spaceships, according to some of the messages. It will occur when earthlings get tuned into the vibrations of the new age.[15]

But contradictions like these are not surprising. Truth is never that important a criterion for those caught up in the intrigue of space-age obsessions.

When Cosmic Cultures Meet

During the last half of the twentieth century, many people around the globe are looking up to the stars, waiting for a landing of the so-called space brothers. Some have even built landing pads. In 1967 in St. Paul, a town in north-central Alberta, the townspeople built a famous one that Mother Teresa visited in 1982. A sign at the pad states in part: "All visitors from Earth or otherwise are welcome to this territory and to the town of St. Paul."[16]

There was also a landing pad built at the town of Lake City, Pennsylvania, near Erie. Arguably the most famous one of all is in El Cajon, California (near San Diego), where the far-out Unarius Academy of Science maintains a sixty-seven–acre landing site, which is supposed to be where thirty-two spaceships will touch down to help bring in the new age. Gracing the site is a large sign that reads "Welcome Space Brothers!" There is a credibility gap with this one, however. In the early 1970s the cult's cofounder, Ruth Norman, announced each year that the landing was imminent and even occasionally set dates (usually around Christmas or Easter) for the landing. Dozens of cult members (and the media) would gather to witness the arrival of the saucers—

which never happened. Finally in 1975 a local television station blasted Norman and her cult and poked fun at the kookiness of the landing extravaganzas, which insulted Norman. The annual date settings stopped[17] in favor of Norman announcing a new final landing date of 2001.[18] If it doesn't happen then, Norman doesn't have to deal with more ridicule. She died in 1993.

Regardless of what New Agers and UFO cultists believe, this leads us to an irrefutable fact. Many people worldwide seem to be getting ready for something big to happen to planet Earth that involves UFOs. Some of this is encouraged by Hollywood and the television industry. The *X-Files, Dark Skies, The Visitor, Sightings,* and other television shows titillate gullible viewers each day in their living room. Not only are more and more people taking this subject seriously, but many people suspect that aliens are already visiting planet Earth. Perhaps this belief was given even more impetus in 1996 when the White House announced scientific findings that there may have been life on Mars at one time. The scientific proof (which has since been vigorously debated by scientists) is strange marks resembling primitive life-forms on a rock, which is thought to have been blasted off from Mars following a meteor strike on the red planet and was found on the ice shelf in Antarctica. In addition, the airwaves and the Internet are filled with talk of conspiracies—even speculations that world governments are already in touch with aliens.

The Crash at Roswell

Near the center of talk about aliens these days is a small city in New Mexico called Roswell, which is the alleged site of a July 1947 flying saucer crash. In recent times this legend has taken on a Hollywood-driven life of its own. It has become so prominent that nearly every American associates Roswell with flying saucers and the alleged crash. In the mid–1990s there was a Showtime cable television special that highlighted the alleged crash near Roswell, and in 1997 the legend was further reinforced by the popular movie *Independence Day.* In one scene of the movie an aide to the president of the United States admits that the U.S. armed forces did retrieve alien bodies and a flying saucer near Roswell in 1947. The saucer is stored in an underground bunker at Area 51 near Las Vegas. It is eventually used to defeat the evil aliens.

In 1997 rumors about the alleged Roswell crash approached a fever pitch. Coinciding with the real U.S. Independence Day of 1997, some community leaders in Roswell (who now have a vested financial interest in keeping the legend of a nearby UFO crash alive[19]) sponsored the Roswell UFO Encounter '97, which was a fiftieth anniversary celebration of the alleged 1947 crash. The event was so well publicized that it made international news, with some magazines such as *Time* and *Popular Mechanics* devoting cover stories to it. On July 4, while NASA's Pathfinder robot landed on Mars and began its extraordinary quest to survey the Martian landscape, CNN cameras kept flashing to Roswell to cover the other space-age event—the bizarre Roswell celebration. Like the Pathfinder, the Roswell event was out of this world in its own right. Among the activities was a flying saucer soapbox derby. Tens of thousands of UFO enthusiasts descended on Roswell for the celebration, with most of them convinced that the U.S. government was involved in a cover-up of the truth concerning at least one crashed flying saucer near Roswell fifty years earlier.

What do serious researchers make of Roswell? Could it be that a flying saucer crashed there in 1947 and was hushed up by the U.S. government? I, along with many others, have looked into this possibility and I believe there is *next to no evidence for these allegations*—and most serious UFO researchers know it. Let us look at the basic facts of the event. On July 8, 1947, "the Roswell Army Air Field issued a press release saying it had recovered the wreckage of a 'flying disk.'"[20] The story was picked up immediately by the wire services and transmitted around the world. But a few hours later an Army Air Force general from Fort Worth, Texas, issued a correction and announced that what had been recovered was the remains of a weather balloon.

The story was then dead until fairly recently, with most folks accepting the official explanation. But now as we are about to enter the new millennium, many new stories about Roswell have emerged, with not one nearby alleged crash site but three of them—with a fourth one well to the west in New Mexico! It seems that as the story is getting older, it is getting more elaborate. Now various legends of Roswell include up to seven tiny alien corpses that were recovered from the site! Indeed, the legends of Roswell resemble the proverbial story of a boy who caught a fish several inches long in the morning, but by the end of the day, after bragging about it to his friends, the fish he had caught was actually more than a foot long!

These Roswell rumors have even taken on cartoonish connotations over time, with some quite willing to suggest other tongue-in-cheek possibilities for at least one crash. For example, in a recent broadcast of *Star Trek: Deep Space Nine,* a shipload of Ferengis from the future, piloted by Quark, gets lost in a time warp and crash-lands near Roswell in 1947! The Ferengis in *Star Trek* lore are a midget race of bald aliens with huge ears that are especially degenerate and greedy, serving as a future race of deep space "pirates" with their own "rules of acquisition" for profit. In the episode titled "Little Green Men," the handful of Ferengis are taken alive by the U.S. Army in Roswell and are examined by medical personnel, while their crashed ship is placed in a nearby hangar. However, all the evidence disappears when the Ferengis escape back to their ship and roar off again into space.[21]

How did the Roswell story emerge from obscurity to become one of the linchpins of UFO belief in the 1990s? Although a historical perspective helps in understanding this, basically, the legend was revived by the UFO enthusiast community itself, which then elaborated on—and perhaps embellished—it. A fact of the matter is that the alleged Roswell crash was practically unheard of in ufology from 1947 to 1978—thirty-one years—until a prominent UFO researcher revived the tale with new details.

Stanton Friedman, a former nuclear physicist-turned-UFO-researcher who now lives in Canada, brought the story back to life. In 1978 Friedman heard the story of the alleged crash and in 1980, following further research by UFO enthusiasts Charles

Berlitz and William Moore, cowrote *The Roswell Incident* that revived interest in the alleged crash.

In 1988 the Center for UFO Studies (CUFOS) sponsored a study of the crash site. Three years later Kevin Randle and Don Schmitt, who had served in the CUFOS investigation, wrote *UFO Crash at Roswell* and alleged that the U.S. government had recovered not only a UFO at the site but also several alien bodies. One of their witnesses was a mortician who claims he received inquiries from the Roswell air base in July 1947 concerning embalming bodies and the availability of children's coffins.[22] Other books adding to the Roswell legend followed, as well as books and articles debunking the myth.

What does the U.S. government have to say about it? They still maintain it was a weather balloon. According to *Time,* "the General Accounting Office announced in January 1994 that it would launch a hunt for any documents related to the 'incident.'"[23] Recently the government said that part of the reason it was not more forthcoming previously about the balloon was that part of its purpose was military. It was known as Project Mogul and part of its purpose was to monitor nuclear tests. The government also said more recently that during the same time period the air force was conducting experiments with dummies that were dropped from weather balloons to examine the impact. Thus it is possible that what some witnesses saw were dummies.[24]

In addition, in 1995 a mysterious alien autopsy film surfaced that has been widely shown on the tabloid television shows, and even some serious television magazine shows. It shows a team of doctors working on a greyish alien-like body. Although the film has been exposed as a fraud by the UFO community and by serious researchers alike, it has served as a subtle encouragement for the public to take the Roswell myth more seriously.[25]

Preparations for the Landing

Some people are so sold out to their belief in an imminent landing of space aliens that they are actually planning what to do when it happens. It was to that premise, that of an imminent landing, that President Bill Clinton was invited to speak at the May 27–29, 1995, "When Cosmic Cultures Meet" conference at the Sheraton Washington Hotel, sponsored by the Human Potential Foundation. Clinton's people expressed his regret at not being able to attend, but many leading figures in ufology were there to try to map out a strategy of what to do *when,* not if, the landing takes place.

Many, citing channeled messages from aliens, said we should welcome the landing, and embrace with gusto the new age the space brothers want to give us. One speaker, James J. Hurtak, Ph.D., founder of the Academy for Future Science, announced to the crowd that there are already "approximately fifty-four different races" visiting planet Earth.[26] Even though some of these races eat humans and mutilate cattle, we should look forward to increased interaction with them, he said! These contact experiences are awakening us, he said. What was his proof that we were indeed being visited?—The word of shamans— witch doctors and other occultists! This is a theme that was echoed by speaker after speaker, some of whom were already allegedly in touch with aliens via trance channeling and automatic writing. There were various shamans at the conference also giving talks on metaphysical themes.

There were only a few dissenters and skeptics at the gathering, and only one evangelical Christian among twenty-three participants giving papers. He was invited to come because they wanted him to fill out the "fear panel"—the discussion group that believes alleged contact with aliens is not a good idea. It was Dave Hunt, author of various Christian books on the cults, occult, and other challenges to the Christian faith. Hunt, a thin, bearded man, who speaks with great passion, gave a masterful talk that sobered the crowd. He challenged them, citing the track record of lies and deception coming from the UFO community and through alleged spirit contact with aliens, to be very wary of any new gospels coming from the stars.

Hitching a Ride to Sirius

The winter solstice was approaching in 1995 and to thirteen Europeans, mostly from France, that meant it was time to die. But because there was so much law enforcement pressure on them, they had to kill themselves in secret. Yes, they would die in a fiery inferno just as other enlightened ones had done who had gone before them. But it wasn't really suicide, they were taught. When their bodies were consumed, they would zoom millions of miles away and wake up on a paradisial planet in the Sirius star system.

In their determination, the thirteen Solar Temple cult members, along with three children they brought with them, tramped through the wilderness in a remote forest in southeastern France to get as far away from contact with the outside world as they could. Some of them had shocked their friends and families by leaving notes behind hinting at suicide. When police found their bodies later on December 23, 1995, they were dumbfounded. The burned corpses were found neatly arranged in a star formation around a campfire. Most had been drugged before receiving one or two bullets in the head, but the three children and one adult did not die willingly, authorities said. There were signs of a struggle. Although all the adult members of the group had made a suicide pact, two of them were former police officers and they were enforcing the pact after the drugs were administered.

It turns out that the Order of the Solar Temple was not the first occult-oriented group to be obsessed with the Sirius star system. In fact occult and UFO literature has long focused on that location as a star teeming with alien life. Many in ufology say aliens from Sirius (whom they often refer to as the Syrians) have already landed on planet Earth. Consider the following.

According to *You Are Becoming a Galactic Human,* an occult and UFO–oriented book by Virginia Essene and Sheldon Nidle, ten thousand beings from more than eight thousand "specially selected star systems" have just arrived on planet Earth to set up the new "galactic human civilization." They're here to help since the planet is still in bad shape from the "energy wars that destroyed both [the mythical lost continents] Lemuria and Atlantis."[1] The landings supposedly started with the arrival of a special Syrian "ambassadorial colony" in mid–1997 and have accelerated. Where did the authors get their information? Through channeling, or spiritism, directly from the Syrians, who are sending us their thought waves from their planet more than eight light-years away.[2]

As strange as it sounds, some people in New Age and UFO circles believe that if the landing hasn't yet happened, it soon will. Sirius has become, according to occult literature over the years, the place from which most alleged aliens and spirit beings come. Its significance can be traced to ancient religion, when it was the object of veneration by the ancient Egyptians, the Zoroastrians, the Australian bushmen, and other groups.[3]

According to Robert K. Temple's 1976 book, *The Sirius Mystery,* which has become a popular favorite among UFO and New Age enthusiasts, the humanoid civilization actually living on a planet circling Sirius is a reptilian race that visited the Dogon tribes of Africa centuries ago. Temple states that the African tribe was actually named after the Syrians, since Sirius is often known as the "Dog star," and is the brightest star in Canis Major, which is one of the constellation Orion's hunting dogs.[4]

Why Shouldn't Sirius Be Important?

There are good reasons for Sirius to have captured the attention of people all over the world for centuries, and they have nothing to do with extraterrestrials. Although it is not the closest star to the sun, it is by far the brightest star in the night sky.[5] It is part of one of the most famous constellations in the sky—Orion, which is even mentioned with awe three times in the Bible, more than any other star (Job 9:9; 38:31; and Amos 5:8). Perhaps, then, an obsession with Sirius is natural. Romans 1:25 talks about humankind worshiping God's creation instead of the Creator.

Occult and ufological speculations about the mythical Syrians have continued for some time. Some have been willing to tell us what these beings look like. At the 1995 "When Cosmic Cultures Meet" conference, James J. Hurtak produced an artist's rendering of a Syrian to illustrate his talk. The Syrian, standing in front of a snowcapped mountain, looks humanoid, except for a large, sloping bald head that juts backward about a foot above his eyebrows. The drawing shows him carrying a strange staff and wearing odd clothing adorned with Aztec-type symbols.[6]

The occult fascination with Sirius can also be traced to Aleister Crowley, the so-called "wickedest man on the earth." Although Crowley has been dead since 1947, he still cuts a larger than life figure in occult folklore. His occult organization, Ordo Templi Orentis (O.T.O.), still continues to operate in cities throughout the United States and Europe.[7] There are other organizations that still follow Crowley's teachings. A member of one of them wrote in 1977, "Jesus shall never return for it was never meant to be. But the Christ, the Logos of the Aeon, the new World Teacher hath come already and his name is Aleister Crowley, the Beast 666."

Crowley claimed that through spiritism, he met an alien from Sirius and he drew a picture of him. Crowley's alleged Syrian,

Lam, looked a bit different from Hurtak's being. Crowley's painting "depicts an eggheaded face characterized by a vestigial nose and mouth and two eyes in narrow, elongated slits," one writer noted.[8] It resembles, except for the eyes, the familiar eggheaded alien often portrayed by Hollywood as a "grey." This type was also portrayed on the cover of Whitley Strieber's best-selling book, *Communion.*

Why should we believe any of these accounts and drawings of the Syrians? We shouldn't. We especially shouldn't believe Crowley, whom some consider to be the most famous Satanist in history. Some have pointed out that Crowley did not believe in Satan's existence, but Crowley did believe in magic, sex orgies, and witchcraft and he called on the devil's name in ceremonies.[9] From his youth he maintained an obsessive hatred of Christianity and he freely practiced mystical rites of other traditions that included Yoga, Buddhism, Cabala, and Freemasonry. He was also suspected of sacrificing animals and even human babies in various occult rituals, according to various sensational writings highlighting Crowley's life.

As far as spiritistic contact goes, Crowley was well ahead of today's UFO channelers. According to his autobiography, *The Confessions,* in 1904, while he spent a night in the Great Pyramid near Cairo, his wife, Rose, fell into a trance, and an entity—an alien spirit that he later called a "guardian angel"—named Aiwas began speaking through her voice. It allegedly told him that he was to create a new religion and that he had been chosen as the new messiah.[10] Later he was given transmissions that resulted in his writing a new bible that he called *The Book of the Law,* which was to supplant all other religions. This book stated that "every man and every woman is a star," and it gave Crowley in a sentence the law that apparently governed his life—unlimited license and hedonism: "Do what thou wilt shall be the whole of the Law."[11]

I have devoted some space to Crowley here because of the fact that he also claimed to have had a link with Sirius, and this has apparently influenced others. Brad Steiger noted that New Age–occult writer Robert Anton Wilson was dabbling with one of Crowley's magic books and decided to perform one of his invocations. The result? He "received an expansion of consciousness" and new wisdom about the universe, and the next day he wrote in his diary "Sirius is very important."[12]

The point is that many occultists and ufologists today have, in the same vein as Solar Temple members, Crowley, Wilson, and others, focused in on Sirius, often after dabbling with the occult. Is this a coincidence or are there real, demonic forces at work helping to spark humankind's interest in particular heavenly bodies?

A Murderous Cult

Luc Jouret, a Belgian-born homeopathic physician, at forty-six had a number of strong beliefs. Among them was the belief that he was Christ. And like Marshall Applewhite, another deluded "Christ" who was teaching his small flock in the American west in the early to mid–1990s, Jouret came to the conclusions that Earth was going to be spaded under and it was time to leave.

Jouret, the French-speaking founder of the International Chivalric Order Solar Tradition, known simply as the Solar Temple, was obsessed with the end of the world and with dying by fire. He amassed a following of about three hundred people at one time in his secret society throughout France, Switzerland, Canada, Australia, and the United States. Some of the followers came to his group when it absorbed another cult, the Foundation Golden Way, which was led by Joseph Di Mambro. "We are in the reign of fire," Jouret said on Swiss radio in 1987. "Everything is being consumed."[13]

Jouret wanted to be consumed as well, along with his people. Long before the horrific series of events began to take place in October 1994, he planned their demise. "As we await a favorable time to return, we will take no part in the destruction of humanity, nor will we leave our bodies to decay in nature's alchemy," he proclaimed in a letter to the world in late 1994. "We will not risk their pollution by enraged madmen. Remember Sodom and

Gomorrah! It shall be the same again!"[14] He then put his plan into motion. They would kill themselves en masse—and thus be rewarded eternal life on a planet orbiting Sirius!

The Solar Temple's View of Sirius

The murderous Solar Temple cult would object to all the previous descriptions of Sirius aliens. No, they're not greys, reptiles, or stately humanoids. They are "etheric" beings—spiritual beings that live forever in a state of bliss. And after the cult members kill themselves in rituals timed to relate to the sun (equinoxes or solstice), they will be whisked away to "reign there forever, weightless and serene."[15]

But unlike Heaven's Gate, they didn't need a UFO to get to the next level. The Solar Temple believed in many traditions, including the doctrines of Ascended Masters made popular by Theosophy. Presumably, other Ascended Masters, or an "Occult Brotherhood," would help them on their way home—but only if they died by fire.

Their passing would be a home going of sorts, Jouret taught. The world had rejected the teachings of the "Occult Brotherhood of 33 Sages" (teachings related to astrology) and the teachings of their disciples, whom Jouret described as "adepts gathered into small secret brotherhoods" worldwide. "Especially in this treacherous passage from the Age of Pisces to the Age of Aquarius has humanity rejected their radiant message," he proclaimed in his "Transit pour le futur" letter.[16] Now the world and all of humanity were degenerating to the point of no hope.

> The global situation has finally slipped out of all human control. Our refusal of accelerated mutation [at the hands of the Occult Brotherhood who were here to help guide the world into the Age of Aquarius] causes degeneration of values in economy, religion, politics, families, society, judiciary. . . .
>
> All Positive and Creative forces are stifled. Man has become a werewolf, preying on his own kind. He can respect neither himself nor Nature, and will eat the bitter fruit of his own decay.[17]

The solution to the decadence is to die. Although people will think it is suicide, it is not. It is really "the Road of Return for a completed Cosmic Evolution." "We refuse to take part in the murder of the Earth that bore us," Jouret wrote in the same letter designed to be read by many after their horrific deaths.

> We withdraw from this world where we can no more be heard.
> . . . Dedicated for eternity to the Kingdom of the Spirit, we have come to Earth to preserve the subtle ties that bind the Creator to the Creature, but now we return to our Home. Throughout our lifetime we have received all the necessary proofs to authenticate our quest. Some people may call what we do suicide, or cowardice in the face of trouble. Others may think of depression caused by the trials each of us has been burdened with. THEY ARE WRONG (emphasis in original).[18]

Seventy-Four Dead in Thirty Months

Obviously Jouret meant what he said. From October 1994 to March 1997, seventy-four people linked to the cult have either been murdered or committed suicide in ritualistic fashion in Canada, France, and Switzerland.

The first wave was the biggest. That occurred on October 5, 1994, when authorities found forty-eight bodies in two villages tucked away in the Swiss countryside. The discoveries began early that morning in Cheiry, a village about forty-five miles northeast of Geneva, when volunteer firefighters saw a burning farmhouse and investigated. After extinguishing the flames, they found blood and a secret doorway leading to the basement. There in a mirror-lined chapel were twenty-three corpses, lying side by side, tied together in a circle with their faces pointing toward a portrait of a Christlike figure that resembled Jouret. "Most had been shot in the head. Some had plastic bags tied tightly around their heads with rubber bands and string. The men wore ceremonial red and black robes, the women long gold gowns. Empty champagne bottles were littered about."[19]

Less than an hour later fifty miles away in Granges-sur-Salvan, an Alpine village near the Italian border, firefighters pulled twenty-five more bodies, including some children, out of the smoldering remains of two chalets.[20] Those fires were apparently set off by a sophisticated wiring device that set the fire when the phone rang.

At the same time across the ocean, "police in Canada were raking through the rubble of a spacious chalet owned by Di Mambro in Morin Heights, fifty miles northwest of Montreal, where five bodies were found. Two were wearing red and gold medallions bearing a double-headed eagle and the initials T.S., for Temple Solaire."[21]

Authorities later said that even though the cult leaders planned to kill themselves, the Canadian deaths were the first ones— and these were sparked by the birth of a child that the leaders thought was the Antichrist, described in the Bible. According to authorities, three-month-old Emmanuel, the son of Antonio and Nicky Dutoit, was ritualistically murdered several days before the fires in one of the Quebec chalets when cult members drove a wooden stake through his heart. The child's parents were murdered at the same time. These murders were ordered by Di Mambro, who thought his daughter, Emmanuelle, was the real "cosmic child" with a sacred future. By naming their son Emmanuel the Dutoits had "usurped her divinity and converted their son into Antichrist."[22]

After those killings, Di Mambro and twelve of his followers had a ritual last supper together, which was followed by Di Mambro and others leaving for Switzerland to join Jouret.[23] Meanwhile, a couple in Switzerland stayed behind to burn down the chalet the victims' bodies were in—and to kill themselves.[24] Altogether during those several days, fifty-three people died, including Jouret and Di Mambro. Authorities later said that of the dead, fifteen inner-circle members committed suicide by poison; thirty were killed by bullets or smothering; and eight were called traitors and were gunned down during the rituals. Some of this group were pumped with as many as eight bullets.

Even though the leaders of the group were gone, their hold on group members continued. It was more than a year later in 1995 when the thirteen adults and three children were found dead in southeast France. The death toll was at sixty-nine.

On March 22, 1997, with the approach of the spring equinox, five more were added by a fiery inferno in a house in Quebec, Canada. They were two French women, two Swiss men, and a Canadian woman. This group had to work hard at dying. At the last minute three teenagers, who were the offspring of members, opted out. *Time* commented:

> For two days and nights before the blast, the grownups had pursued a remarkable will to die. Over and over they fiddled with three tanks of propane that were hooked to an electric burner and a timing device. As many as four times, they swallowed sedatives, then arranged themselves in a cross around a queen-size bed, only to rise in bleary frustration when the detonator fizzled. Finally, they blew themselves to kingdom come. For them that would be the star Sirius.[25]

Experts are divided over whether there will be more Solar Temple deaths. But as a result of what has happened, there have been calls to outlaw the cult in France, and the French government has responded by tracking "fifteen doomsday cults" it says are operating in the country. Police in various parts of the world are also keeping a close eye on known Solar Temple members or associates. Press reports indicate that police are alerted to the potential for fiery deaths with every equinox or solstice.

Pressures on the Solar Temple

Some law officials and cult experts point out that the Solar Temple had become very unstable in the year leading up to the suicides, due to vigorous prosecutions against the cult. Among the pressures were accusations of financial wrongdoing and money laundering and charges from former members that the cult was engaging in frightening mind-control practices against its members.[26] Additionally, as was the case with the Branch Davidian group in Waco, Texas, law officials were becoming alarmed by reports of the cult stockpiling weapons.

But the Solar Temple was far different from the Waco group. While the Branch Davidians had their roots in Adventism and a perverted form of Protestant Christianity, the Solar Temple's roots were in Freemasonry, Rosicrucianism, secret societies, mythical Roman Catholic Knights Templar beliefs (that included a belief in the Holy Grail and a search for the ark of the covenant), rounded out by astrology and the New Age beliefs. In contrast with the Branch Davidians, the Solar Temple group was also well connected socially and financially, as many prominent and wealthy people were on the rolls of the dead. Some members gave the group multi-thousand dollar cash contributions.

Although Jouret and Di Mambro talked about their alleged links in a previous life to the Knights Templar, those links, of course, did not exist. The Knights Templar was "originally a group of nine crusaders who pledged in about 1118 to lend their services to the protection of Christian pilgrims to Jerusalem," writes Ted Daniels of the Millennium Institute. "The Order succeeded quickly, grew wealthy, and won renown for its military feats. Eventually they became Europe's money lenders, a position that led to their persecution and eventual anathematization and extermination in 1314."[27]

What then did they believe in? Anything and everything, it would seem. But Ted Daniels puts it this way:

> Jouret's teachings borrowed from three main streams: the eco-cide predictions of many New Age believers; the notion of a cosmic *"renovatio"* revealed by the Ascended Masters (Ams) to their neo-Templar successors, and extremist political notions of a final ideological apocalypse, from various left- and right-wing groups Jouret stayed in touch with.[28]

But it is also obvious, from reading much of Jouret's literature, that he thought he was in touch with a number of entities and he received various revelations—including a "final revelation" that led to death. That was: "between 1993 and '94, the last 'guardians' of the planet would leave for higher realms." His revelations emphasized four "sacred objects": the Holy Grail, King Arthur's mystic sword Excalibur, the menorah, and the ark of the covenant.

Like many other occultists, Jouret was obsessed with specific occult sites on earth, including the Great Pyramid in Egypt. He claimed that there were seven "'entities' hidden in the Great Pyramid." When the entities left, it would signal the end of the world.[29] They left on January 6, 1994, he claimed in a letter.[30]

Some believe that societal and governmental pressure may have been factors in the Solar Temple's eventual demise.[31] This was the case with the People's Temple cult and the Branch Davidian group; however, isn't it the government's function to protect its citizens by monitoring groups that pose a potential threat? I believe government not only has the right to monitor these groups, but it has an important duty to perform in doing so. There are some (including the apologists for the cults), however, who argue that the cults become extremely paranoid and irrational when placed under the investigatory spotlight and they would argue for less government "interference" with such groups. I would argue that it was the behavior of the cults in Guyana and in Waco that drew the attention of officials. It was similar for the Solar Temple. Before the first waves of fiery deaths, *many* people with loved ones in the group were becoming upset by Jouret's teachings and were urging government intervention. Their concern increased especially when Jouret became steadily more fixated on the end of the world and was publicly urging his followers to stockpile weapons. The *Philadelphia Inquirer* explains:

> In 1993, Jouret was charged with conspiracy to obtain illegal firearms. . . . The case centered on Jouret's attempt to purchase a handgun with a silencer, which he said he needed for personal protection. It received enormous media attention. Some stories speculated that the cultists were preparing for Armageddon. . . . Other accounts linked the Solar Temple with a group of terrorists that had threatened the lives of two Cabinet ministers.[32]

During the uproar, police tapped Jouret's phone and listened in on a conversation in which Jouret told a woman to begin learning how to use a gun and to not tell anyone about it. He later pleaded guilty to a conspiracy charge, paid a one-thousand-dollar fine, and

91

left Quebec, where he had lived for a few years, for Switzerland.[33] But in Europe the heat remained on him when Swiss, French, and Canadian officials probed the possibility "that Jouret and Di Mambro had been involved in gunrunning or money-laundering schemes," and there were even unproven accusations that surfaced that "Solar Temple leaders had purchased guns and other military equipment in Australia and resold the material in the Third World."[34]

In a letter sent to a Swiss expert on cults just after the first wave of deaths, an apparent survivor of the death ritual blamed the media, the government, the courts, and the police "for forcing us to leave this earth" because "noble action" had become impossible.

Additionally there was evidence that the cult was losing members, due in part to negative publicity, and at the end "the group was down to no more than one hundred" members, according to an expert on the group.[35]

Many Antichrists

This book deals with some of the many space-age delusions that are becoming evident as we head into the new millennium. Many of them are led by people who claim to be the very Christ of the Bible. These groups are cropping up worldwide, in dozens of cultures and settings. In many cases these false christs are hypnotically leading large and small groups of people into insular communities. Even during the writing of this book, I have learned of new religious leaders almost every day who are claiming to be Christ on the one hand, while they are talking about UFOs or outer space themes on the other. As we have seen, some of them are capable of convincing their followers of just about anything, including killing others and then themselves. It is truly a frightening time.

Can mass suicide happen again? I believe it can. In Russia there are several self-proclaimed christs talking about suicide and the end of the world. One of them, according to *Time* magazine, is a former police officer named Vissarion. "With his flow-ing dark hair, wispy beard and a sing-song voice full of apho-risms, he has managed to attract about 5,000 followers to his *City of the Sun*" in Siberia. He tells them that suicide is not a sin.[36]

And there is also a female christ—the leader of the White Brotherhood cult—Marina Tsvigun, who calls herself "Maria Devi Khrystos (Christ)." Tsvigun was given a prison term along with other leaders. "The group urged followers to gather in Kiev for Judgment Day, which they said would fall on November 14, 1993. The cult's leaders were arrested when the foretold apoc-alypse did not occur."[37]

According to the November 5, 1993, Radio Free Europe report on the Kiev incident, there were five hundred cult members detained. The White Brotherhood followers had "flocked into the capital for the celebration of 'God on earth' and the resur-rection of its leader, Maria Devi Khrystos." The report added:

> The celebration, which was to be marked by the end of the world, the collective suicide of the cult's followers, and the ascension of Khrystos into heaven. . . . The cult's followers are mostly young people in Russia, Moldova, Belarus, Uzbekistan, and Ukraine; in Kiev alone there are 2,200 adherents.
>
> So far the cult has been accused of 143 cases of swindling and 199 cases of squatting, and has been charged with encouraging suicide.

Despite the jailing of the cult's leaders, the cult was "agitat-ing in St. Petersburg" (Russia) the following year as they were handing out portraits of their leader. They also set a new time for the end of the world—at the beginning of the next century. Tsvigan was released from a women's correctional labor colony in August 1997.[38]

Similar movements bear watching elsewhere as well, not to mention various radical Islamic groups abounding worldwide, looking for the return of the Mahdi. This is an imagined Shiite messianic figure who some Moslems claim has been sleeping inside a mountain for centuries until the time is right for him to return and conquer.

In Thailand a guru heading the Sri-ariya cult claims to be the master of heaven in the "Millennium Kingdom." His followers greet each other with Nazi-style salutes and refer to each other by the names of past Thai kings. Police raided the cult's headquarters in 1995.[39]

Is it a coincidence that Jesus said that just before his return religious deception would be so great that it would threaten to deceive even his followers? "For false christs and false prophets will arise and show great signs and wonders, so as to deceive, if possible, even the elect," Jesus said (Matt. 24:24).

Science Fiction Armageddon

Ten thousand years into the future, Hari Seldon is trying to save the galactic empire from falling into a new Dark Ages. Unless he acts fast, the empire may take thirty thousand years to rebuild.

It is *Star Trek* to the extreme; it's a federation of twenty-five million planets spanning across the galaxy ruled from Trantor, a planet of forty billion souls, so overcrowded that its surface is totally covered with human structures extending a mile deep into the ground. Nature doesn't exist anymore in this world, except at the emperor's palace where the surrounding grounds are rich with trees and flowers.

Seldon knows of the coming collapse and disaster, because unlike the remote viewers of the twentieth century, he has discovered how to see into the future with complete accuracy through a technique he calls "psychohistory." He warns the government of what he sees: endless interstellar wars, a decline in trade, a population decline, and the empire breaking apart. But they're not interested. So he takes matters into his own hands to save the federation.

This is, of course, science fiction. Chances are that you are already familiar with the story because it is science fiction at its best. The author is the late Isaac Asimov, one of the most talented and prolific writers the world has ever seen, producing 502 books. The premise of the just-painted galactic opera was the basic story line for his seven-book *Foundation* series, one of the most famous science fiction series ever written, and arguably the best one ever written. In fact the first three books of the series, *Foundation* (1951), *Foundation and Empire* (1952), and *Second Foundation* (1953) were given a prestigious Hugo Award in 1966 as the best all-time science fiction series.[1]

Blueprint for Armageddon

Asimov, the Russian-born, American writer, didn't envision that his *Foundation* series would become the plan, the blueprint, for a dangerous Japanese doomsday cult that would try to kill millions of people in a failed bid to bring on Armageddon and a new millennium. What was the force behind this cult, known as Aum Shinri Kyo (Supreme Truth)?

Chizuo Matsumoto, a partly blind man, who worked as an acupuncturist and yoga instructor, allegedly became "enlightened" during a trip to meet holy men of the Himalayas in 1986, and a "message from God" came to him. According to David E. Kaplan and Andrew Marshall's book *The Cult at the End of the World,* the audible voice said to him: "I have chosen you to lead God's army." He then changed his name to Shoko Asahara and declared himself Christ on Earth. Japan would never be the same.[2]

At his peak he had more than forty thousand devotees in six nations, about ten thousand in Japan and a small number in Europe and North America. But the bulk of his members came from Russia, where, just after the collapse of communism, he rushed in to fill the spiritual void experienced by people who had been told since childhood not to follow spiritual things. One of the highlights of his life was in March 1992. While he held a rally before nineteen thousand Russians at Moscow's

Olympiski Stadium, a giant video screen flashed images of Asahara being Jesus Christ crucified. He sat on a throne in center field observing it all while the gathering was told about his ability to go for an hour without breathing.[3]

To be sure, Asahara also claimed to be "the Buddha of our times" and he had a background in Buddhism, rather than Christianity. But after he read through the Bible for the first time he said, "I hereby declare myself to be the Christ. . . . I am the last messiah in this century."[4] He even wrote a book titled *Declaring Myself the Christ*. And he meant it too. He claimed he could perceive past lives (in one previous incarnation he designed Egypt's pyramids)[5] and read people's minds. He could even levitate, pass through solid walls, and meditate for hours underwater, he said, claiming that in the future he would be able to fly through the air as the legendary Superman.[6] Scores of people with a lot of money believed every word, and an extraordinary number of young professionals, including scientists, doctors, and lawyers, joined the cult and formed Asahara's inner circle. According to Kaplan and Marshall:

> Drinking the guru's blood was one of twenty so-called "initiations" the cult now offered. Holy Hair Initiation was a bizarre variation on the traditional Japanese tea ceremony, wherein snippets of Asahara's locks were brewed in boiling water and then drunk. His beard clippings were also on sale ($375 per half-inch). . . . Asahara now repackaged his dirty bathwater as "Miracle Pond" and sold it for nearly $800 per quart. There was "Nectar Water"—tap water blessed by Asahara which supposedly glowed in the dark.[7]

They even bought his semen, published reports noted. Why not? He hobnobbed with the Tibetan god-man, the Dalai Lama. He was scheduled to be the leader of the world, the first of a race of "superhumans" following the soon-to-come apocalypse. He would be the one, through his superior teachings, to repair the world following the coming catastrophes. He was even more than willing to place dates on the coming terrors.

Although many UFO cults and space-age groups are apocalyptic, most of them view UFOs and their occupants as "friendly," wanting to help guide planet Earth into the new millennium. Asahara didn't buy it. He said UFOs were nasty, a sign of Armageddon, and he linked UFO sightings to the coming of Halley's comet. He also said that aliens were real and that they killed people, eating them "like human soup." UFOs will become "one of the main factors of Armageddon," he said, and they are boarded by beings from higher levels of consciousness.[8]

Asahara set dates for supposed future events but they kept changing, depending on his latest visions from extraterrestrial sources. He said that Japan would be a virtual police state after 1990 as the result of trade friction with the United States (it didn't happen); that Japan would sink into the ocean in 1996; that the end of the world would begin in 1999; and by 2003 Europe, the United States, Russia, and China would fall. And between October 30 and November 29, 2003, nuclear war would almost totally obliterate humanity.[9] The only way to avert disaster was to become his disciple and spread his cult, Aum Supreme Truth, throughout the world. "Then we can avoid World War III for sure," Asahara said. "I guarantee it."[10]

Now, however, Asahara, who repeatedly said that he admired Adolf Hitler, is accused of trying to *start* World War III. He is accused of planning at least twenty-seven murders, including the deadly sarin gas attack on the Tokyo subway system on March 20, 1995, that killed twelve and sickened fifty-five hundred people. Sarin is a toxic nerve gas that was used by the Nazis during World War II. Asahara was also a suspect in a gas attack at Matsumoto that killed seven, as well as of other attacks that could have resulted in a greater loss of life, including a failed attempt at gassing the Japanese parliament. Apparently he was attempting to build an atomic bomb. In addition, *Time* noted:

> Aum researchers were trying to develop germ weapons—including the Ebola virus—and an assembly line was about to produce automatic rifles. Behind one [Aum] building's false walls was a $700,000 lab able to turn out 60 to 80 kg a month of the nerve gas sarin—enough to kill 6 million to 8 million people. One plan called for releasing the sarin over Tokyo from 1.65-meter-long remote-controlled helicopters. Asahara would follow up the

attack by overpowering the Japanese Self-defense Forces and taking control of Japan with his own tanks and fighter jets.[11]

Two hundred Aum cultists were arrested and are awaiting trial for their role in the attacks. The Aum religion was banned in Japan, and the trials could go on for up to ten years in Japan's slow judicial system. Asahara, who was not arrested until more than a month after the Tokyo subway gas attack, could get the death penalty. He was captured while hiding in a secret chamber at the cult's headquarters.

How does this relate to Asimov's science fiction world? In Asimov's *Foundation* universe, after Trantor leaders reject Hari Seldon's vision of the future, he decides to take matters into his own hands and save humanity himself. This is done in the series of books as characters hop from planet to planet (including one called Sirius), working with life-forms, and, in the later books, working with robots as well. The way to save humankind was to do exactly what Asahara attempted to do in Japan: Create a secret society comprised of the "best minds of his time—the scientists, historians, technologists—and, like monks in the Middle Ages, they set about preserving the knowledge of the universe."[12] In Asimov's fiction, Hari Seldon wanted to control the future. He organized this secret society, called the Foundation, into a religion.

Just as he predicted, Hari Seldon died, but his scientist-priests were considered wizards and holy ones, and therefore the religion that Seldon created was used to control men and worlds and to guide the future. Hideo Murai, Aum's Minister of Science and Technology, who was the architect of the cult's weapons program, said Asahara was using the *Foundation* series as a blueprint for Aum's long-range plans. "Shoko Asahara, the blind and bearded guru from Japan, had become Hari Seldon; and Aum Supreme Truth was the Foundation."[13] And the over-populated Trantor corresponded to Japan, the most densely populated nation on Earth.

Some speculate that part of the reason Asahara wanted to start Armageddon was, in his own twisted reasoning, to ensure that there would be more survivors coming out of a future world war. What he meant was that if Armageddon were launched now, instead of at a later time when hostile world powers would amass even more destructive capabilities, more people would survive to help rebuild the world (presumably following his leadership) after the apocalypse. Under this reasoning if Armageddon were to be unleashed now instead of later, many more people would be "rescued"! "If Aum tries hard, we can reduce the victims of Armageddon to a fourth of the world's population," he preached. "However, at present, my rescue plan is totally delayed. The rate of survivors is getting smaller and smaller."[14]

Others have speculated that he had mixed motives; another reason Asahara moved on the subway system was old-fashioned hatred and crazed paranoia. After all, the voters of Japan had resoundingly rejected him in his earlier bid for an elected office in Japan, and he felt spurned by that. Additionally he knew that multiple investigations were forming, both in Japan and internationally, targeting him and his sect. The word was out that police were on the brink of launching a raid on his Mount Fuji compound.

Asahara's Control

As is the case with members of many other cults, people who joined Aum Supreme Truth cut off most contact with their families, as the cult wanted them to do. This, of course, angered many parents because they lost all contact with their children.

Asahara wanted total control of his followers. Their diet and sleep were controlled twenty-four hours a day, as was their brain—*literally.* Members were fitted with what the cult called "hats of happiness," headsets that regularly delivered strong electric shocks to the head. Adult members received 6 volts to the brain at regular intervals, while children received 3-volt buzzes. These electric shock treatments were called the PSI, Perfect Salvation Initiation, and were designed by Aum Supreme Truth "scientists" to help devotees' brain waves be synchronized with Asahara's brain waves. But it was, of course, actually pseudoscience and potentially dangerous electronic quackery. The hats did nothing but inflict Aum followers with a steady stream of pain, while draining their wallets. Full-time cult "monks" were given the shock hats for free. But they were rented to others for seven thousand dollars a month, or sold outright to devotees for about seventy thousand dollars![15]

Aum and Scientology

In recent years police around the world have been honing in on another cult linked to science fiction mythology. It's the Church of Scientology, founded by the late science fiction writer L. Ron Hubbard. Some experts have drawn parallels between Scientology and Aum Supreme Truth. One of the differences between these two space-age groups is that Scientology has a much larger worldwide following.

Let's look at some similarities between these two cults linked to science fiction:

- While the Aum group has its PSI shock caps that have no proven medical benefits, Scientology has its e-meters. On January 4, 1963, the U.S. Food and Drug Administration raided Scientology offices and seized hundreds of e-meters as illegal medical devices. These electrical devices are designed to be used by an "auditor" to determine the level of a member's engrams (which are negative in Scientology's theology). Since the raid, the e-meters are required to carry a disclaimer on them stating that they are purely a religious artifact.

- Japan has outlawed the Aum group, and numerous countries, including Germany, are attempting to outlaw the Church of Scientology.

- The Aum group has been repeatedly accused of using mind control techniques on its members. So has Scientology.

101

- The Aum group has been repeatedly accused of harassing Japanese government officials. Scientology has faced similar accusations from governments in various countries, including the United States.

- Aum members have faced mass jailings in Japan. Scientologists have faced mass jailings in various settings, including Italy in January 1997.

- Aum has been linked to suicide and death. Scientology has as well. In fact the head of the Lyon, France, branch of Scientology was jailed and fined for his role in the suicide of a member.

- Aum was very litigious, suing its critics at will, including the Japanese government. Scientology has filed dozens of lawsuits against the U.S. government, the Cult Awareness Network, and its critics, including the media.[16] Although not many of these suits have been successful, with many of them being thrown out of court, they have cost the critics of Scientology millions of dollars and untold heartache.

I could make many other parallels, but one of the most intriguing is the connection between the two religions and the science fiction fantasies that helped spawn them. Scientology is a space-age cult. It is replete with references to life on other worlds, aliens, galactic rulers, and an intrigue between good and evil, the same stuff L. Ron Hubbard's space fantasy books were about.

Hubbard, who was a prolific science fiction writer, has his own series of books similar to Asimov's *Foundation* series. They are the ten-volume *Mission Earth* books and are sold by Bridge Publishing, a subsidiary of the Church of Scientology. They talk of secret intrigues and invasions involving the earth nations and the dealings of a galactic empire, and in each book a hint of the theology that was to become the Church of Scientology shines through. For example, in *An Alien Affair,* volume four in the series, a weapons salvo is lodged at Earth and it is told it cannot exist partly because the planet condones immoral behavior, and that leads to the practices of "psychiatry" and "psychology."[17]

Fortune of Fear, volume five, is touted as "a deadly trail of action across Turkey, through the Mediterranean, into Swiss banks and a mafia-controlled casino as two alien forces struggle to determine the fate of Earth and control of a galactic Empire."[18]

The Birth of Scientology

Although Isaac Asimov, who was Jewish, sometimes wrote against organized religion and even tried to explain away Christianity, few, if any, people believe he wanted to start his own religion. According to published reports of his life, he worked on writing projects from 7:30 A.M. to 10 P.M. daily and may not have even been aware of Asahara and the Aum cult. Hubbard, however, intended to start his own religion, and part of his reasons may have been financial.

Speaking before a writer's conference in New Jersey in 1949, Hubbard said, "Writing for a penny a word is ridiculous. If a man really wanted to make a million dollars, the best way would be to start his own religion." The next year he did. That's when his book *Dianetics: The Modern Science of Mental Health* was published. Although this book became the foundation stone of the church, it was immediately criticized as being Hubbard's concoction, part of a moneymaking scheme to begin building a personality cult fashioned around his legacy.

As do other groups I discuss in these pages, Scientology projects outer space mythology directly into its doctrine. A Spiritual Counterfeits Project fact sheet on Scientology reports this:

> Ultimate reality, Hubbard has come to teach, is populated by "Thetans," or gods—eternal, uncreated, omnipotent, omniscient, personal beings, free from all laws, all cause-effect relationships, and all other Thetans. However, by collective agreement, the spiritual Thetans submitted to one another and created the Material-Energy-Space-Time (M-E-S-T) universe external to themselves.[19]

Later these Thetans reincarnated into the bodies of animals and plants and eventually evolved into man. However, by the time man appeared, the omniscient Thetans forgot about their divine heritage and they had to be awakened. In the 1960s Hubbard added new twists to his religion: The Thetans were actually banished from their universe seventy-five million years ago by a "cruel galactic ruler named Xenu" and forced to live on Earth. A Scientologist who wants to follow his religion faithfully has to audit those Thetans (for a large monetary fee) so he or she can eventually achieve a state of "clear," which is equivalent to the godhood promised by New Agers.[20]

Ralph Lee Smith, writing in *Today's Health,* said that this Thetan

had inhabited the body of a doll on the planet Mars, 469,476,600 years ago. Martians seized the doll and took it to a temple, where it was zapped by a bishop's gun while the congregation chanted "God is Love." The Thetan was then put into an ice cube, placed aboard a flying saucer, and dropped off at Planet ZX 432, where it was given a robot body, then put to work unloading flying saucers. Being a bit unruly, it zapped another robot to death and was shipped off in a flying saucer to be punished. But the flying saucer exploded, and the Thetan fell into space.[21]

The serious student wishing to go higher in Scientology would also have to have some "body" Thetans released, which are negative spiritual beings that have "been asleep or unconscious inside you for millions of years." Total cost for the step-by-step process, according to *Time:* two hundred to four hundred thousand dollars.[22] What's more, *Time* and a number of publications have pointed out that at the highest level of Scientology, the highest truth that one can know is that L. Ron Hubbard is God. Church of Scientology officials would not confirm it, but if this is what they believe, would it surprise anyone?

Before Hubbard founded his church, he was an active member of Aleister Crowley's Ordo Templi Orentis branch in Los Angeles. He also, according to Kenneth Grant, Crowley's successor as head of the O.T.O., was the "first modern occultist to demonstrate the existence of superior alien intelligences." Grant also noted that Hubbard was somehow connected with subsequent extraterrestrial contact.[23] He also claimed in other lifetimes to have visited Venus, the Van Allen Radiation Belt, and heaven twice.[24]

Belief in Reincarnation

Another area of convergence of Scientology with the Asahara cult is the belief in reincarnation. As we have already mentioned, Asahara claimed to have lived previous lifetimes and even claimed credit for designing the Great Pyramid of Giza, Egypt. We have also seen that Applewhite and Nettles of the Heaven's Gate UFO cult were also believers in reincarnation. Actually almost all space-age cults hold to the New Age belief of reincarnation—that they have lived before and will live again in another form after death. This is a basic belief of Hinduism, which is the worldview that has influenced most UFO cults. However, as we have seen, each space-age cult has its own twists of doctrine. For example, many UFO cultists believe that at death they will be reincarnated into another human life-form or one equal to a human, such as a space alien.

But the reincarnation concept in India is a little different than that of Western-styled cults. There it is referred to as transmigration and it means that coming back as a human is not guaranteed. It depends on the way one behaved in working out one's karma in a previous life. Therefore, if one does not do well, that person may come back as a lesser life-form, like a rat or even an insect, such as a fly, or even in a nonlife-form, such as a rock. That is why cattle are revered in India. They are thought to house advanced souls who've learned something after many incarnations. Cattle are closer to the final step—Nirvana, a state of endless bliss—in the universe.

What's so wrong with this? UFO enthusiasts ask. After all, many New Agers teach, reincarnation was at one time in the Bible but was later taken out by the church. I've heard this argument many times from UFO enthusiasts and New Age believers at conferences and at speaking engagements throughout America. But the fact of the matter is that the doctrine of reincarnation was *never* in the Bible, and both Old and New Testaments strongly teach against it (see Heb. 9:26–27). There were no church councils or secret meetings anytime in history that ordered the Bible rewritten and that doctrine expunged. Furthermore, historical documents prove that there were never any rewrites, revisions, second editions, or cutting out of *any doctrines* of Christianity. Nevertheless, this lie that the Bible has been altered is widely believed by occultists today.[25]

Reincarnation is a clever way of getting rid of the sacrificial death of Jesus on the cross for the sins of the world. If we are going to be reincarnated to work out our bad karma from a previous life, why then do we need a Savior who has paid for our sins? Hebrews 9:27–28 states, "It is appointed for men to die once, but after this the judgment, so Christ was offered once to bear the sins of many. To those who eagerly wait for Him He will appear a second time, apart from sin, for salvation." No, we don't come back another time.

Daniel, in the Old Testament, also knew what to expect following death, although the Old Testament concept of hell was different than what came later following the resurrection of Christ. Daniel was given a vision directly from God on it and it wasn't reincarnation. He knew the choice was heaven or hell: "Many of those who sleep in the dust of the earth shall awake, some to everlasting life, some to shame and everlasting contempt" (Dan. 12:2).

David too, in the Book of Psalms, remarked that we don't return after death as the New Agers and Hindu-oriented groups teach: "For He remembered that they were but flesh, a breath that passes away and does not come again" (Ps. 78:39).

FLYING SAUCER MESSIAHS

French race car driver Claude Vorilhon says that when aliens return to earth in a flying saucer to help usher in a new world order by 2025, they will land in Jerusalem. In advance of the landing, Vorilhon, who claimed that in December 1973 he was renamed Rael by aliens from another world, has been raising money to build an embassy and a landing pad in Jerusalem for them, whom he calls the Elohim.

The Israeli government since the mid–1980s has refused permission for him to build, and since then it has not stated if it ever will grant him permission. Chances are it won't. Vorilhon has faced scandal in his native France and elsewhere amidst lurid reports that his Raelian Movement, an international UFO cult that claims thirty-five thousand members in eighty-five nations,[1] has been involved in free love and group sex as part of its religious dogma. Vorilhon, however, defends the practices, calling them sensual meditation.

Another reason for Israel's reluctance may be Rael's claims that he is the messiah for this generation, the Christ—and it is he who will be on the throne as the "guide of guides" for the world from Jerusalem when the aliens come back.[2] In fact Vorilhon claims that he, along with Jesus, Moses, Mohammed, Joseph Smith, and other great "prophets," as he puts it, are the sons of aliens.[3] Vorilhon says his French mother was abducted by aliens on December 24, 1945, and the next day—Christmas day—was impregnated. (However, "the aliens wiped her memory clean," he said. "She believed one of her boyfriends made her pregnant."[4])

Perhaps another reason the Jewish state is not allowing Vorilhon's Jerusalem building project to begin are nagging suspicions that his cult is anti-Semitic. Rael has claimed that when the saucers come down, the aliens' insignia will be prominently displayed on each spacecraft—a large swastika inside a Star of David! But Vorilhon protests these suspicions. The Raelian Movement is not sympathetic to the Nazis, he says. Their swastika is not like the Nazi symbol. It actually "represents the infinity of TIME," according to a Raelian booklet widely distributed in the early 1990s.[5]

Vorilhon, a bearded, curly-haired man who often dresses in white and is escorted by beautiful, scantily clad young women, has been willing to be flexible concerning the symbol. This flexibility has been characteristic of religious cults over the centuries when they have come under fire. Vorilhon has changed the symbol so that it is more palatable.[6] According to the sect's Web page, this change did not come as the result of revelations from the space brothers:

> In February year 46 after Hiroshima, Rael decided to change the symbol of the Raelian Movement and replace the swastika with a galaxy which, like the swastika, represents the cycle of infinity in time. This was done out of respect for the victims of the Nazi holocaust and to facilitate the building of the Embassy in Israel, despite the fact that the Elohim's symbol is the oldest on earth and that traces of it still remain in Israel today.[7]

Susan Jean Palmer, who took a scholarly look at women in the Raelian Movement in James R. Lewis's book, *The Gods Have Landed,* also talks about some of the rituals practiced by the cult.

Denying the existence of God or the soul, Rael presents as the only hope of immortality a regeneration through science, and to this end members participate in four annual festivals so that the Elohim can fly overhead and register the Raelians' DNA codes on their machines. This initiation ritual, called "the transmission of the cellular plan," promises a kind of immortality through cloning. New initiates sign a contract that permits a mortician to cut out a piece of bone in their forehead (the "third eye"), which is stored on ice awaiting the descent of the Elohim. The initiates are also required to send a letter of apostasy to the church in which they were baptized.[8]

Otherworldly Encounters

Vorilhon, who was a journalist for the French magazine *Racing Car,* claims that as he was driving his car near Lyon, in central France on December 13, 1973, he felt a compulsion to turn toward an isolated dormant volcano, a short distance from the city. While walking in the crater of the volcano a "bell-shaped" UFO approached him through the fog, and a small "green-skinned" humanoid with almond-shaped eyes jumped out to talk with him.[9] He claims that the space being chose him as the one to spread "the greatest message ever revealed to humanity" and that he would be an apostle of a new world order.[10]

Jacques Vallee, one of the most influential UFO investigators, gives a negative view of Vorilhon and his movement in his book *Messengers of Deception.* He says Rael's goal is very clear—to be the spiritual ruler of the world. Vallee notes that Vorilhon has written that the Elohim told him that they "want us to destroy democracy after selecting as a prophet a man born in France"—himself![11]

As the story goes, he met with the aliens six times and on October 7, 1975, he met with the Elohim again and spent twenty-four hours with them. Eventually they took him to their planet where he met Jesus and Satan. Vorilhon's revelations are put forth in two of his books: *The Message Given to Me by Extra-terrestrials* (1986) and *Let's Welcome Our Fathers from Space* (1986).

The message was that he was to prepare humanity "for the Age of Apocalypse to the Age of Revelation," which was kicked off by the explosion of the first atomic bomb in 1945. The space being also told him that life was created by aliens from the Elohim planet in a DNA laboratory.[12] According to Raelian theology, the monotheism of people from the Judeo-Christian tradition is wrong, and it is a mistake to refer to God in the singular. What we have been mistakenly referring to in the singular is the Elohim, which in reality are many space aliens who helped create humanity.

Vorilhon, who seeks to "demythologize" Scripture, insists that the Bible is really the history of a space colonization.[13] He claims that he is the last of forty prophets throughout the centuries, and his job is to raise the planet's consciousness so we can "inherit the scientific knowledge of our space forefathers." He also said that 4 percent of the human species will clone themselves and travel through the universe, populating virgin planets "in our own image" in the future.

Meeting Jesus

Since he was born as the result of a virgin birth—as was his alleged half-brother Jesus of Nazareth—Vorilhon claims to be the messiah of this generation. According to Vorilhon, he had an emotional meeting with Jesus when the aliens took him to their world—the planet of the Elohim. (According to one report, Vorilhon doesn't know exactly where that planet is, except that it is outside our solar system, yet in our Milky Way galaxy. He says the Elohim, who are capable of travel faster than the speed of light, also inhabit a second planet.[14])

Vorilhon wrote that while on the Elohim planet, he met an alien named Yaweh, who told him that after the Hiroshima atomic attack, "we decided that the time had come for us to send a new messenger on Earth." They then selected a woman "as we had done in the time of Jesus." The woman was Vorilhon's mother, who was artificially inseminated by the aliens.[15]

According to the story, Yaweh, his eyes filled with "a great emotion and feeling of love," then turned to Vorilhon and said:

"From this moment on you may call me father, because you are my son." Jesus was also there, and he was emotionally moved as well. "Then I kissed my father and my brother [Jesus] for the very first time."[16]

Meeting Satan

Vorilhon also claims that he met Satan on the Elohim planet. The Bible warns that Satan is "our enemy" and is "like a roaring lion, seeking whom he may devour" (1 Peter 5:8). The Bible also calls him Satan, the devil, "the father of lies" (John 8:44 NIV), the evil one, the one "who leads the whole world astray" (Rev. 12:9 NIV), and a variety of other unflattering titles. But Vorilhon says the Bible has misunderstood Satan. The devil is actually a good guy, "the bearer of light" who first revealed to humankind that the gods were not divine but simply people like themselves.[17] Satan was also a scientist who helped create humanity in a laboratory, Vorilhon says.

Other Raelian Beliefs

Vorilhon's Interpretation of the Bible

Not surprisingly, Vorilhon warps the Christian message in one of its most vital points, the core of Christian doctrine—Jesus' death on the cross and his resurrection. Vorilhon has added on to the Bible to give us an alternative account of the life of Christ and his purpose on earth. He has also added variant readings of some of the biblical stories, including the creation story.[18] Jesus *was* actually crucified on a Roman cross, says Vorilhon, but he was later scientifically revived by other aliens and taken back to the Elohim planet. He didn't die for the sins of the world, Vorilhon declares. In *The Message Given to Me by Extra-terrestrials,* Vorilhon said that Jesus' purpose on earth was to help us advance scientifically and medically to make room for the return of the Elohim to the planet.[19]

But now, a little more than ten years after that declaration, Vorilhon has a new spin on Jesus' crucifixion. He has altered doctrine just as he changed the cult's symbol. Jesus wasn't revived; he was cloned, the "new Jesus was actually a clone of the original one."[20]

This is preposterous. If the resurrected Jesus was simply a clone of the real one, then why were there nail prints in Jesus' hands after the resurrection? Jesus offered Thomas, the disciple, an option of thrusting his hands into the spear gash in his side and touching the nail prints in his hands (John 20:27). This denial of the truth of the Bible is typical of UFO cults. My investigation reveals that all UFO cults, in one way or another, alter the person, nature, and work of Jesus Christ. By altering his mission and his death on the cross, UFO cults reduce his message, which destroys the truth. The resurrection of Jesus is truly one of the most important doctrines for Christians. The apostle Paul put it this way: "If Christ is not risen, then our preaching is vain and your faith is also vain. . . . And if Christ is not risen, your faith is futile; you are still in your sins! Then also those who have fallen asleep in Christ have perished. If in this life only we have hope in Christ, we are of all men the most pitiable" (1 Cor. 15:14, 17–19).

Eternal Life for Two Hundred Thousand Dollars

Cults often counterfeit Christianity. That is why one of the leading Christian apologetics ministries to the cults and occult in North America has taken the name Spiritual Counterfeits Project.[21] I am bringing this up because the Raelian Movement now has a clever counterfeit for Jesus Christ's offer of eternal life. Jesus gives it to us free, but there's a price for the eternal life Vorilhon offers. It costs two hundred thousand dollars and of course there's no guarantee that his scientists and cult doctors can pull it off *through cloning!*

In a world where almost all civilized nations are condemning any attempt at human cloning and are rapidly passing laws against such Frankenstein-type experiments, Vorilhon claims to have set up "the first human cloning company." According to a Raelian press release, the apparent successful cloning of a Scottish sheep named Dolly was the impetus to set up the company called Clon-aid. The company offers parents insurance that covers the accidental death of their children. The company will simply make another child. For fifty thousand dollars the company will "provide the sampling and safe storage of cells from a living child in order to create its clone if the child dies of an incurable disease or through an accident."[22]

Here is Vorilhon's way to eternal life: "Cloning will enable mankind to reach eternal life. The next step, like the Elohim with their 25,000 years of scientific advance, will be to directly clone adult people without the growing process and to transfer memory and personality. Then we wake up after death in a brand new body like after a good sleeping night!"[23]

Living as a Raelian

Vorilhon obviously doesn't have a very high regard for human life. He is also short on chaste behavior and does not affirm the traditional family. The accepted behavior within the Raelian Movement includes abortion on demand[24]; the right of women to be unmarried mothers, single mothers, and sexually active single mothers; the right of women who get sick of their children to dump them[25]; a discouragement of marriage; and encouragement to dump one's spouse when tired of him or her.[26] Homosexuality and lesbianism are also rampant within the cult, and there is a large number of "strippers, transvestites, and highly expressive homosexuals among the congregation," noted Palmer.[27]

Vorilhon wants his followers to enjoy life and have sensual pleasure. Perhaps this is why he is embarking on an entertainment building project in addition to the Jerusalem embassy project. He wants to build UFO Land, a theme park devoted to UFOs. Fund-raising has begun for the project, to be built in Valcourt, Quebec, Canada, east of Montreal.[28]

Speaking of sensual pleasure, Vorilhon claims that one of the ultimate goals of his movement is to experience the "cosmic orgasm." He claims he was guided in that area during his trip to the Elohim planet where he was given a choice of six beautiful robot women who were created to fulfill his sexual fantasies. Vorilhon says that when he couldn't decide which woman he wanted for his companion, he took all six and "spent the most extravagant night" of his life with them in his alien hotel suite.[29]

It's little wonder then that his followers follow suit. Annually cult members participate in a sensual meditation workshop "in a rural setting which features fasting, nudity, sensory awareness exercises, and sexual experimentation."[30] Press reports call them yearly orgies.

Another San Diego UFO Cult

The Heaven's Gate cult was the upstart UFO cult in the San Diego area. The UFO cult that has been there for many years is the Unarius Education Foundation. Like the Heaven's Gate cult, they too have talked a lot about future events. The Unarius group doesn't teach that the earth will soon be spaded under, as Applewhite taught. They teach the opposite: Flying saucers are coming to bring the earth into a glorious new age. They have little patience for some Christians too. Those who think that the Antichrist of the Book of Revelation in the Bible will come to lead the world to ruin are the evil ones, according to the El Cajon, California–based group. These people are "left-hand path workers" and are "in alliance with the demonic forces who are working against the truth," an undated Unarius booklet states.[31]

In that respect, the Unarius group, which is one of the most colorful UFO groups of all, generally agrees with Vorilhon—there's no Antichrist coming, just the spaceships. In another respect Unarius would thoroughly agree with Vorilhon's statements that Satan is really an alien, and a good one at that. But while the French race car driver affirms that Lucifer has always been good, even helping to create us using DNA in a laboratory experiment, the Unarians say he was once a bad guy who has totally conformed to goodness. He is now a Way Shower:

> The soul Satan, Lucifer and Jaweh, who had many other names, has factually been overcome, has seen the error of his ways and

actions and has joined the FORCES OF LIGHT, TRUTH AND GOOD. . . .
Satan has given up, he has exchanged his strong ego and erro-
neous beliefs for Truth, and now is a servant or server of the
Light! So fear no longer this evil-doer! He no longer does evil
works but rather, he channels Light—clear and pure and has
become a Way Shower![32]

As previously mentioned, in 1967 the space brothers allegedly
told Ruth Norman, the cofounder of the cult, to prepare a landing site "for the arrival of thirty-two city-ships from the Intergalactic Confederation."[33] She then bought sixty-seven acres of
land east of San Diego, where she put up the sign "Welcome
Space Brothers." She said that at least some of the aliens would
be from the Pleiades constellation (another popular origin point
in UFO folklore). According to Norman and her followers, the
rolling hills of the California site would be no problem. The
aliens would simply "laser blast the hills to create level ground,"
that is after "a pleiadean starship will land on a rising portion
of Atlantis in the area of the Bermuda Triangle in the Caribbean
Sea in the year 2001!"[34] Besides, near San Diego, the aliens won't
need as much space as one may think. They are scheduled to
land on top of each other, attaching and forming a towering gigan-
tic city. Each ship will contain one thousand scientists that will
fan out across the globe and help solve humankind's problems.[35]

Is This a Joke?

The Unarius Foundation's beliefs and unusual publicity-seeking
events are embarrassing to some in the general UFO movement.
Its members are often seen as oddballs and even kooks. This was
encouraged by Norman's predictions of flying saucer landings in
the 1970s and continues because of their annual colorful Interplanetary Confederation Day and the Interplanetary Conclave of
Light ceremonies. During these ceremonies, which are a cross
between a parade and a pageant, Unarian members dress up in
the bizarre costumes of alleged alien civilizations about to visit
Earth.

115

Channeling Jesus

Ruth Norman, unlike most of the other UFO cult leaders in this book, never claimed to be Christ. She claimed *only* to have been betrothed to Jesus in a previous life (as his girlfriend, who she says was Mary Magdalene in Israel) until Jesus was wickedly hung on a cross. But she finally caught up to Jesus in 1954 when she met Ernest Norman at a psychic convention, and this time he didn't get away—she married him. You see, Ernest was Jesus in a previous life. But when they met, they didn't know that he was Jesus Christ in a previous life and that she was Mary Magdalene.[36] That came later after "Ernest started to receive transmissions from on high." In previous lives, Ruth Norman claimed to have been Socrates, Peter the Great, Charlemagne, Queen Elizabeth I, and Queen Maria Theresa.[37]

But Ernest, known as the "Moderator of the Universe," died in 1971 and since that time has moved on to live as Jesus on Mars[38] where he continues to guide the cult through channeling to his beloved Ruth, who also died in 1993. So, although Ruth Norman sought more publicity than most of the cult leaders mentioned in these pages, she was perhaps not as pompous as Vorilhon or Asahara or other christs. She never claimed to be Christ. That was her late husband. She only claimed to be the *only* channel through whom the Moderator of the Universe could flow to the earthlings![39] She was also "THE NEW SPIRITUAL WORLD LEADER now living on the Earth world—incarnated especially to help bring in this NEW AGE OF SPIRITUAL RENAISSANCE—THE AGE OF LOGIC AND REASON!" (emphasis in original).[40]

Attacking Jesus

Like other UFO cults, including Heaven's Gate, the Unarians have savagely attacked the person, nature, and work of Jesus, as well as the Christian church. Channeled books that are offered for sale by the Unarius Library include *Reflections of My Life: The Apology of John the Baptist,* in which the one who baptized Jesus in the Jordan River two thousand years ago allegedly apologizes (through channeling) for his great sin in his past life of advancing "Jesus as the Jewish Messiah." "This recognition, was for the author, a great healing, freeing him from the insanity of this past-life," the Unarius advertisement says.[41]

The library also includes the apostle Paul's channeled confession (through Ernest Norman) that Christianity was altered. The Christian religion is the culmination of a "villainous plot, contrived by the arch-villain Saul of Tarsus and his cohort, Judas Iscariot; a plot that changed the world's history for thousands of years." The book also has Paul, from the grave, denying the virgin birth of Jesus by exposing for the world "who his mother and father were." This book, the Unarius advertisement trumpets, "exposes for all time the great hypocrisy of the Christian religion."[42]

It's not surprising that Unarius teachings also deny the second coming of Jesus Christ. According to the 1984 booklet *Easter Message from Jesus of Nazareth (Now Archangel Raphiel)* that was allegedly channeled via Ruth Norman on April 22, 1984, there will be no second coming of Jesus in the flesh. Instead, the second coming is in the form of the Unarius cult. The booklet, as well as many other Unarius documents, denies Christ's death on the cross and his resurrection. Unarians add to God's Word by giving this variant rendering:

> Jesus did not die on the cross! The governor, Pontius Pilate, permitted Nicodemus, who came to him, to purchase the corpse. Jesus had not succumbed before they were able to get Him down from the cross. He was carried quickly to the tomb Mary had purchased for her father.
>
> Several of His close friends helped to resuscitate Him, using alloys and herbs, which took Him about three days to recuperate.
>
> It was no great event for such an Advanced Master as is Jesus— and we keep that in the present for He is indeed alive and well, thank you, on the Inner Planes; in fact, He is the prime mover and leader of Unarius—to mentally move aside the huge bolder that barred the entrance of the tomb! When He was sufficiently strong to walk, He left the tomb and lived for six months, when the wounds in His hands and side caught up with Him, through infection. The poison finally killed Him . . . the Greatest Light!— but only in the physical!

We tell these truths to especially help the religionists who are unfamiliar with these facts.[43]

I am especially unfamiliar with these facts, because to make a statement like this is about as solid as the idea that there was a spaceship trailing the Hale-Bopp comet. It is a demonic lie, intended to void Jesus' sacrificial death on the cross and his resurrection, which is the basis of Christianity itself.

A New Leader

There is now the question of how much longer the cult will survive. Ruth Norman, who guided the cult through many of its odd antics, died on July 12, 1993. Although the cult's Web page claims a worldwide following of half a million,[44] Diana Tumminia and R. George Kirkpatrick's scholarly study of the group indicated a mailing list of five thousand and only sixty-five people show up for important events. The sect's Academy of Science, which meets at their headquarters in El Cajon, had forty-seven students in 1992.[45]

Since Ruth Norman's passing, leadership of the sect has swung to Charles Spiegel, an alleged "expert" in "past life therapy." Indeed, a belief in reincarnation, both of humans and aliens, forms a central plank in the cult's doctrine, along with the belief in channeling spirits. Most members act out in colorful detail in pageants their alleged past lives. Spiegel, a longtime Unarius devotee, has also authored some of the Unarius books, including ones allegedly channeled from dead people. His most famous one is *Confessions of I, Bonaparte.*

The "Messiah" Who Fell to Earth

Once upon a time as a comet buzzed by the earth, the messiah of the new age dropped down to help the needy planet. Come to think of it, it wasn't that long ago when it happened, according to a rapidly growing UFO cult. The time was 1970 and it was a flying saucer trailing Bennett's comet that did the trick. Never heard of this comet? It was highly regarded by astronomers. It had a yellow tail that shone brightly in the night, so much that "some Egyptians feared it was an Israeli secret weapon."[46]

According to the rapidly growing, semisecretive cult headquartered in Eatonton, Georgia, the new savior of the world came to planet Earth "like a thief in the night" from the planet of Rizq, one of nineteen planets from the nineteenth galaxy called Illyuwn. This cult is called the Holy Tabernacle Ministries or Ancient Mystical Order of Melchizedek.[47]

Their "messiah" is an African American named Dr. Malachi Z. York. That's his name for now. At previous times, back in Brooklyn, he went by the name Amunnnubi Rooakhptah, and later when he identified himself as a Sufi Muslim teacher he went under the name Imam Isa.[48]

York matter-of-factly describes his trip *back* to earth from the vicinity of the comet—because he has been here before. "In order to get here I traveled by one of the smaller passenger crafts called SHAM out of a motherplane called MERKABAH or NIBIRU," he explained.[49] "I manifest into this body to speak through this body. I am an Entity, an Etheric being." He claims the body he is in is that of a mustachioed and bearded man who was born June 26, 1945.

"I have seen worlds come and go where I come from beyond the stars, a planet called Rizq," he said. ". . . Now I am sent here to beings who think I'm crazy. However, I will still do my job. . . . I know you think I'm nuts, but in time the whole world will know I am here and who I really am," York confides.[50]

Who does he say he is?

"I am the lamb, I am the man," York declared in a message dated November 16, 1996. "I am the supreme being of this day and time, God in flesh."[51]

His followers who, as the Heaven's Gate cult did, have a large presence on the Internet, would heartily agree. They call him "the Master," "the Savior," "papa," "the Lamb of God," and other names reserved for deity. An oft-repeated slogan found on multiple Internet Web sites produced by cult members is: "Peace in the Lamb, It's Truly Wonderful!" Some of the group members' Internet sites

119

have flying saucers whirling about on the computer screen. Many sites gush about York. Consider this one:

It was His time to come in flesh . . . with the power as the Sun of Righteousness with dark reddish brown skin color, hair like lambs wool and eyes like flames of fire. You could not stare in his eyes long before you felt him looking down inside of you. He is warm and happy. Yet you see a deep sadness in his eyes for he knows he must save.[52]

He teaches his far-flung group, according to the cult's literature, that they can, through his teachings, elevate themselves to godhood. "Thus you can say, I am that I am," he declares.[53]

In previous incarnations York claims he has been known by other titles including Christos (Christ), Y'shua, Jesus, Adonai, Melchizedek, the Islamic Mahdi, Elohim, Yaanuwn (Teacher of the Universe), Al Hajj Al Imam Isa (Teacher of Islamic Hebrew), and a number of other titles often used for God or gods in other religions. He is also Malachi who "may strike the Earth with utter destruction," he claims.[54] He has also called himself Chief Black Eagle, and one photograph released by the cult shows him in full Native American headdress. He claims to be associated with an ancient mound-building tribe in Georgia to which he attaches special religious meaning.[55]

Earth to Be Spaded Under

York has much in common with Applewhite of the Heaven's Gate cult. Just as Applewhite claimed to be Jesus Christ and urged his spiritually in-tune followers to leave the planet with him on UFOs, so does York. York would also agree with Applewhite's belief that the earth is being spaded under. But his details differ. York's scenario includes evil extraterrestrials who, in league with various earthly agents, conspire to kill 75 percent of the world's population through AIDS and other calamities:

Your planet is full of resources and it is conducive for many life forms in the universe. Some extraterrestrials want to live here,

120

while others want the natural resources and will return to their planet. In order to achieve this, they have to eliminate 75 percent of the world's population. They are doing this through AIDS for the sexually promiscuous people, and with drugs, music and alcohol to sedate you. They call this recreation, which in actuality is wreck-creation.[56]

Only those who follow York will survive, he says, laying out his doomsday scenarios more specifically. He says that on May 5, 2000, when the major planets Earth, Mars, Jupiter, and Saturn line up with the Sun, there may be a "star holocaust" that will pull the planets toward the sun.[57] Then one hundred forty-four thousand worthy souls will be picked up from earth by spaceships in the "rapture." York explains:

> At the same time the crystal city also called the Mothership that comes from an even bigger craft called Nibiru, the Motherplane, Merkabah meaning The Moveable Throne, will release the passenger crafts called Shams to pick up the worthy souls. It will take three years for the Shams to reach the planet Earth from the asteroid belt. . . . Then August 12, 2003 A.D., this is the opening of the vortex that will allow the crafts to come through. June 26, 2030 A.D., this date is the last pick up date for the 144,000.[58]

Structure of the Cult

Although York began his teachings in Brooklyn where he was linked to Black Muslims and occult spiritism, he considers Georgia "the Mecca" for Nubians (those with African ancestry) that dominate his group. Accordingly, the cult is "developing an Egyptian-styled city, including three pyramids, on a 400-acre tract," ten miles northwest of Eatonton, Georgia, which serves as the cult's headquarters.[59]

Besides the group's extensive presence on the Internet, they have bookstores where they promote their teachings and sell many of York's booklets. They have also set up "lodges," regional meeting places. The Watchman Fellowship in Birmingham, Alabama, which is an evangelical ministry to religious cults, said the sect has bookstores throughout the southeast. They also have a presence in the northeast, including the Baltimore-Washington area and Brooklyn.

Although there is a lot of positive talk about Jesus in the cult's literature, York is decidedly anti-Christian. He denies the bodily resurrection of Jesus following his crucifixion; only his soul was resurrected, he says. He slams the historic Christian doctrine of the Trinity; he slams the Bible,[60] slams Christians, claims the apostle Paul "was merely a glory seeker,"[61] and blasphemously declares that Jesus "had two wives"—Mary and Martha.[62]

York's teachings contain many contradictions. His religion is a synthesis of many religious traditions—including a smattering of astrology and New Age occultism along with strong Islamic overtones. While he condemns the Bible, he also affirms some of it and reinterprets it, often turning the meanings upside down. With unabashed blasphemy, York claims the title of the Lamb of God, because he says the Book of Revelation identifies him as the worthy Lamb of God who is able to open the scroll.

Actually, the Bible in the Revelation passage is clearly talking about Jesus Christ of Nazareth, the one crucified on a Roman cross outside Jerusalem two thousand years ago, as the only one able to open the scroll and unleash judgment on the world. It will also be Jesus who will pronounce judgment on York and the Ancient Mystical Order of Melchizedek.

Jesus of Nazareth is the true Lamb of God, as the Book of Revelation says. It is Jesus who is clearly identified as the one who was "pierced" (Rev. 1:7) and as the Lamb who "had been slain" (Rev. 5:6). It is also the Lamb, Jesus, who will cast the Antichrist and the false prophet into the "lake of fire burning with brimstone," partly because the Antichrist caused the world to worship him, and the false prophet backed him on it (Rev. 19:20). This is precisely what York demands of his followers: worship.

"For false christs and false prophets will rise and show signs and wonders to deceive, if possible, even the elect," Jesus said, in describing the state of the world just before his return (Mark 13:22).

I have seen many photographs of York. There are no nail prints in York's hands. His side has not been pierced by a Roman spear. He has not fulfilled any of the messianic prophecies. He is not only erratic, but he's spiritually dangerous. According to "Our Story!", a document placed on the Internet by the cult describing its history, his doctrines have changed many times since the 1960s. He has been into occult spiritism for a long time and claims to possess "eight distinctive personalities," some of which are "Extra-terrestrial beings."[63] He is a Sibyl in disguise, hearing from the other side and following the same general script as Marshall Applewhite.

FLYING SAUCER DECEIVERS

UFO cults often don't agree with each other. Take the case of George King, the founder of the Aetherius Society, for example. He sharply disagrees with the Unarius Society's pronouncements, advanced by the late Ruth Norman, that Jesus is now living on Mars.

Instead, says King, Jesus is living on Venus.

King says he knows this because on July 27, 1958, he met him. Jesus, walking out of a spaceship that landed on a hill, gave him "the first chapter of His Aquarian age Bible to Earth,"[1] a text King called *The Twelve Blessings* that serves as some of the primary teaching of the Aetherius Society today. He has since received many "transmissions" from Jesus (via trance channeling) and from another being from Venus, Aetherius, after whom the society is named.

The Society, which is now headquartered in Los Angeles, was founded in 1955, making it one of the oldest UFO cults in existence. Claimed membership is several thousand, according to the sect. It also has a European headquarters in London and claims offices in Auckland, New Zealand; Ontario, Canada; South Africa; Nigeria; and Ghana. It is one of the most colorful groups with a mystical worship system. During ceremonies—sometimes on hilltops and mountaintops—members may don robes and hold their palms to a machine in solemn chanting, which they call dynamic prayer.[2] For years King has been a regular at many UFO conventions wowing crowds with his onstage channeling of beings from other worlds, delivered as he wears dark goggles.[3]

King won't be at more UFO conventions. On July 12, 1997, during the writing of this book, King died. Since his death, his cult, the Aetherius Society, has remained active and has an advanced Internet Web site.

In some ways it is little wonder that King claimed Venus as a special place inhabited by spiritual aliens riding in flying saucers. In UFO lore coming out of the 1950s (less than a decade after what ufologists say was the start of the modern UFO era in 1947), no planet has been cited more than Venus as the origin of UFOs. In that decade dozens of contactees surfaced, all claiming to have either met or been in contact with aliens from that planet. Venus remained a center of attention into the early 1960s, when Russian and American space probes were sent to that clouded planet to discover that the atmosphere enveloping it was filled with poisonous gas, trapping it in tremendous heat. In the early 1990s the U.S. space probe *Magellan* mapped Venus's surface and reported it as a planet with a jagged rocky surface and hellish temperatures approaching 900 degrees. It is little wonder that following scientific revelations about Venus in the 1960s, it was almost uniformly dropped by contactees and channelers as the home of friendly aliens.

Because of this and other scientific advances, few UFO enthusiasts now look to Venus as the place from which most aliens originate. However, Mars seems to be making a comeback. It too was popular in the 1950s as an alien origin point, but that popularity fizzled after a *Mariner* probe in the 1960s beamed back photographs of the red planet and showed it riddled with impact craters and revealing no life. That was further confirmed by the soft landing of two NASA Viking craft on the surface in 1976, which also reported inhospitably cold temperatures. But in the wake of reports in the mid–1990s of possible signs that primitive life once existed on Mars, coupled with the interest NASA's roving Pathfinder robot has stimulated following a July 1997 landing, UFO enthusiasts are once again choosing Mars as the origin point of alien life (at least there was life there at one time, multiple channelers and remote viewers tell us!). Mars is favored also because of reports of a face formation on the planet's surface, Martian pyramids, and even the remains of an alleged city in the Cydonia area of the planet.[4]

George King also talked of life on Mars. In his 1950s book, *You Are Responsible,* he speaks of his alleged out-of-body trip to Mars, where he was wounded by a dwarf toting a ray gun. Later he wrote that he helped the Martians destroy an intelligent meteorite with "a weapon of love" that was attacking their space fleet!

In some ways, King was a throwback to the 1950s. His claims that the alleged UFOs visiting Earth are inhabited by benevolent aliens who are helping guide the planet into a new age and that most aliens come from our own solar system are themes not shared by most ufologists today.

Aetherian Beliefs

The story of the Aetherius Society started in 1954 when King, a London taxi driver and an ardent Yoga practitioner, claimed that he heard "a loud and clear physical voice" declare to him inside his London flat: "Prepare yourself! You are to become the voice of Interplanetary Parliament." The thirty-five-year-old King was, according to an Aetherius Society biography sheet, "shocked by the implication of the statement. . . . George spent many sleepless nights, consulted with advanced Guides [through channeling] from the higher realms, as well as reaching within to try and fathom the implications of this Command."[5]

A week later on a Sunday afternoon, "a great master of Yoga from India" walked through a locked door and into his flat. That contact enabled him to make telepathic connections with Aetherius, the being from Venus.[6]

The theology of the group evolved into a mixture of astrology, reincarnation, Kundalini Yoga, Eastern mysticism, and occult channeling, mixed with King's own doctrines—which he claimed came from aliens. He said that Jesus, Buddha, Krishna, and other religious leaders were of extraterrestrial origin and they came to Earth to help humankind.

King developed other distinctives over the years, including the invention of a do-nothing machine—the radionic machine. He said the machine stores the earth's prayer power in batteries until the power can be released. Like Scientology's e-meter and Aum Supreme's PSI shock caps, the device does nothing beneficial, yet it is essential to the Aetherius Society.[7]

Although King was among the few UFO cult leaders mentioned in these pages who did not claim, in one way or another, to be an incarnation of Jesus, he claimed to be in touch with Jesus telepathically. He claimed to be *the* voice of the interplanetary parliament; "the Cosmic Masters of the Solar System began using Sir George King as Primary Terrestrial Mental Channel," Aetherius literature states.[8] His seventy-eighth birthday, January 23, 1997, also marked the beginning of the new age, the Society says.[9]

King's transmissions, more than six hundred of them allegedly from space (and a few other places in between), also serve as the background of new divine revelations to planet Earth. Since King claimed that the Bible has been altered over the centuries by the Christian church, his channeled revelations are locked in underground vaults in Los Angeles and London "so that future generations will not have to rely upon the . . . inaccuracies of second-hand reporting of great events." "Imagine if we had a videotape of the Sermon on the Mount," an Aetherius Society official told the *Los Angeles Herald Examiner* in 1983. "This is the equivalent."[10]

The Holy Mountains

In many ways King's religion is legalistic and mechanistic. One of the curious practices of the Aetherius Society is Operation Starlight, which King said the Cosmic Masters have called "the most important single metaphysical task ever undertaken upon earth in this, Her present life." Operation Starlight has to do with nineteen mountains that have allegedly been spiritually charged by King between 1958 and 1961. "While on these mountains, he entered into an elevated state and an initial Charge was sent through him," states an Aetherian document that explains Operation Starlight. "Each mountain was then fully Charged with Spiritual Energy by the Cosmic Masters. This Energy is now available to all who expend the effort to climb these mountains to send out their prayers and healing."[11]

Subsequently these nineteen mountains, the power points for planet Earth, are the site of annual Aetherian "Holy Pilgrimages." Therein lies the contradiction. If these are the power points for the entire planet, then why are the overwhelming number of the so-called Holy Mountains situated near King's followers in *English-speaking countries?* Nine of the mountains (which would be considered small hills to some living in mountainous regions, such as the American West) are located in Great Britain, four of them are in the United States, two are in Australia, one in New Zealand, one in Switzerland, one in France, and one (Mount Kilimanjaro) is in Africa. No mountain peaks are included from the magnificent Himalayas, the Andes in South America, the Urals in Russia, the mountains of Japan (including Mt. Fuji), and numerous other ranges in non-English-speaking lands.

The New Age Christ

Central to the Aetherian belief system is that a New Age Messiah is coming to planet Earth and he won't be Jesus Christ. He will be greater. He will be wearing what appears to be a space suit and he will rule the world. King said that he received in 1958 the following "Cosmic Prophecy" from an extraterrestrial known as Lord of Karma. In part it says:

There will shortly come Another among you. He will stand tall among men and a shining countenance. This One will be attired in a single garment of the type now known to you. His shoes will be soft-topped, yet not made of the skin of animals. He will approach the Earth leaders. They will ask of Him, His credentials. He will produce these. His magic will be greater than any upon Earth—greater than the combined materialistic might of all

129

the armies. And they who heed not His words, shall be removed from the Earth.[12]

In discussing further this alleged coming world ruler, King's cult strongly affirms an apocalyptic scenario that is taught by many UFO cults, but is the opposite of what Heaven's Gate taught. The Aetherius Society believes that those who won't go along with a coming new age will be removed from the earth. Aetherian literature is very specific on this, but not so specific on when it will happen. "Within ten years or it could be a hundred years. It depends on mankind's progress." Here are some details about the new age and its ruler:

This Master will arrive on Earth in a spacecraft, openly. Unlike previous Cosmic Masters such as the Master Jesus, the Lord Krishna and others, he will be allowed by Karmic Law to use his great powers. There will be no question of who he is and where he came from.

The coming of this Great Avatar will be a pivotal point in the New Age. After his coming, those who are not ready to go forward into the era of Light—the New Age, will slowly be removed from the Earth to be reborn on another less evolved planet. They will then continue to learn through experience, only under much more difficult conditions than are now present on Earth. All who are ready will stay upon Earth and join together to build for themselves the much prophesied New Age.[13]

A Warning

As a longtime researcher of the cults and the occult I have learned to be suspicious of the claims coming from these religious systems. Sometimes they lie. Often they are braggarts who make unwarranted, fantastic claims they can't back up. Some are masters of making false predictions and prophecies. Already in this book I have documented some of their deceptions.

The Bible teaches that followers of Christ are not to puff themselves up in any way. They should not brag about any accomplishments. Through the infilling of the Holy Spirit, they should be pointing to Jesus and what he has done on the cross rather than to man. Likewise, the Holy Spirit never calls attention to himself. Jesus said that when the Holy Spirit comes he will "convict the world of sin, and of righteousness, and of judgment" (John 16:8). This is in direct contrast to the UFO "messiahs" and "prophets" of today! Notice in these pages how many of them call attention to themselves, claiming to be the spiritual leader of the world (and sometimes the universe as well).

What I mean is that just because many UFO enthusiasts and New Agers are talking about a tremendous leap into the new age and about the coming of a great world leader, we shouldn't expect these things to happen. The Bible tells us to test all things and hold fast to the good (1 Thess. 5:21). We should look with spiritual discernment at any of the claims, comparing their statements with what the Bible teaches, as the early Christians in Berea did (Acts 17:11).

We should also be aware of the fact that the Bible tells us of satanic signs and wonders (and even power) coming through false prophets and messiahs just before the real Messiah, Jesus, returns (see 2 Thess. 2:9–10 and Matthew 24). Many Bible scholars also believe that Revelation 17 discusses the rise of a great worldwide false religious system coming in the same time frame. Although not all Bible scholars agree, many believe that coming also during that era will be a false leader who will "devour the whole earth" (Dan. 7:23; 11).

Could ufology and the fascination with aliens be a piece of a puzzle of worldwide religious deception? Remember, UFO interests are not just confined to the United States and Western Europe. It is a *worldwide* movement that is even more deeply rooted in Third World countries. Ufology is huge in Russia and the nations that were part of the former Soviet Union. Interaction with beings from space is an obsession with Native American tribes, Eskimo tribes, and in African and South American shamanistic worship systems. (As I have shown, ufology is directly related to New Age spiritism and shamanism.) "The descent of sky gods to marry earth goddesses," is a theme much reinforced in the Shinto worship system in Japan (where ufology is big business).[14] Likewise, in the ancient *Bhagavad Gita,* which is one of the primary texts of Hinduism, there are references to beings from other realms coming to earth.[15] And Hollywood, with its constant UFO and science fiction lore, is affecting the entire world, for there may not be a more homogenizing force in the world than television and the Hollywood film industry.

Some Christian leaders have entertained the idea that the coming Antichrist referred to in the Bible could claim to come from a flying saucer and dazzle the world. Indeed, I have discovered that many premillennial Christian leaders are at least willing to discuss this possibility. Some have even talked about a possible great alien conspiracy against humankind in these "last days." Many others, however, think this is far-fetched. The late Dr. Walter Martin openly speculated before his death:

> Suppose the sign of antichrist is not to appear in normal fashion, but instead, to be a technological saviour, not a spiritual saviour. A Superior technological intellect, a supernatural being with all power, signs and natural wonders. Suppose he could cause the deserts to be irrigated and end famines. Supposing he could impose a benevolent despotism upon the world and stop national fighting and squabbling about boundaries. . . . Supposing he could give us cures for cancer, AIDS, herpes, diabetes, arterial diseases. Suppose this super technology presented us with signs and lying wonders. Do you think the world would build him a temple and worship him? I do. I think they'd go to Jerusalem on their knees and kiss his feet, because the world isn't looking for a spiritual redeemer.[16]

A Famous Swiss Contactee

Although the Swiss Eduard "Billy" Meier claims he doesn't run a worldwide UFO cult, he has many critics who contend that he does. They say Meier's teachings, which he claims were given to him by aliens, are religious and that people worldwide are following him.

No one disagrees that the Billy Meier story, or legend as some call it, has greatly impacted ufology today. The story that has grown around him over the years is that he has taken many clear photographs of UFOs and that he has been in repeated contact with beings from the Pleiades star system, 450 light-years away. He even claims to have been taken aboard their spaceships on various occasions.

Meier has argued that he does not run a religious cult because he is often a loner and does not hold regular services or very often teach publicly. On the other hand, his teachings about UFOs and his contacts with alleged aliens are religious in nature and are decidedly anti-Christian as they have undermined the person, nature, and work of Jesus Christ. Whether or not the elderly Meier is in charge of anything personally these days is in a sense, though, irrelevant. The fact is that people around the world have organized around him and they have based their religious beliefs on his teachings and his alleged revelations from aliens. Perhaps the largest group linked to Meier's teachings is an organization called FIGU.[17] This organization, which directly subsidizes Meier, maintains a headquarters called the Semjase-Silver-Star-Center in Schmidruiti, Switzerland, Meier's hometown. FIGU claims that it is not religious in nature but this is questionable. On the Swiss nonprofit organization's Web page there are fifty belief points, most of which are religious in nature, akin to New Age occultism.[18]

Meier, who is at the center of what some call the "best documented UFO case ever,"[19] has produced hundreds of clear photographs of alleged UFOs that he calls "beamships" from the Pleiades. Some of the shots show a handful of ships hovering over the Swiss countryside. They have appeared in UFO literature worldwide, as reporters and film and television journalists from as far away as Japan have descended on Meier's rural home in Switzerland, writing news features on Meier.

Since his story is so well known throughout the world, some of the lore from his alleged contacts has caught on in New Age–UFO circles everywhere. For example, many people today are claiming to be channeling or having direct contacts with Meier's alleged primary contact, Semjase, a beautiful blonde female ufonaut, who is allegedly more than three hundred years old.[20] Meier was also the first to popularize the Pleiades—a star cluster

133

sometimes known as "the seven sisters"—as an origin point of UFOs. Now this constellation, more than 400 light-years away, is one of the most popular ones that alleged aliens derive from.

Despite his worldwide notoriety, however, most groups in the UFO community consider Meier a fraud. One author called his story "the most infamous hoax in ufology." Dennis Stacy, editor of the prestigious *Mufon UFO Journal,* wrote that "photographic analysis [of Meier's photographs] . . . reportedly revealed that Meier's amazing array of flying saucers consisted of small models suspended from strings."[21] In 1995 Prometheus Press, a secular humanist publishing house, produced a 439–page book, *Spaceships of the Pleiades,* that presents Meier as a fraud and a liar who produced fake photographs of UFOs. The book also states that Meier claims to be the reincarnation of Jesus Christ, but FIGU denies that.

Many others have questioned the Meier story. Gary Kinder has reported in his book *Light Years* that Meier's then wife, Popi, became angry and confessed her role in having helped perpetuate what she said was a long-running UFO scam. She showed a European investigator slides, which she allegedly pulled out of a fire, showing models of Pleiades beamships that Meier made and superimposed on prints of the Swiss countryside.[22]

In another case Meier announced that Semjase, the beautiful Pleiadian, took him on a beamship trip into the future and allowed him to take a photograph of San Francisco as a heap of ruins following a huge, future earthquake. However, the picture he proudly displayed was a fake; the same picture was actually a painting that appeared later in *GEO* magazine. It was an artist's lifelike painting of what a massive earthquake might do to the city.[23] Meier is accused of plagiarizing it.

Meier also drew snickers from various UFO investigators with his claim during a beamship ride to have met God in outer space and photographed his eye![24]

Because of the facts that have caused most researchers to brand Meier a fraud, it is not my intention to get into extensive detail on this case.[25] But I will pay some attention to it for several reasons. First, I want to show how this group, formed around the most famous contactee in the world, has a decidedly occult and anti-Christian agenda. Second, and perhaps more interesting as it relates to the purposes of this book, I want to show how doctrines develop—and sometimes rapidly change within the UFO community. I believe Billy Meier's UFO tale in the late 1990s has dramatically changed from its original form. I will also show that those who are still pushing the Billy Meier legend have a financial stake in keeping it alive. They want to continue using the Meier name to make money. In other words, there is evidence that the Meier story has been drastically altered to further the financial interests of those in line to make money from it. This coincides with what I have discovered during my probe of the UFO movement.

Billy Meier and the Semjase-Silver-Star-Center in Switzerland have put the little town of Schmidruiti on the map. Numerous international camera crews have been through the Swiss town, highlighting scenes from the countryside and town for the whole world to see. This has resulted in increased revenue for the community. Numerous celebrities, including Shirley MacLaine, have visited Meier over the years. Thus the community has become Roswellized in a sense. As I said earlier, although there is no strong evidence that any flying saucers have crashed near Roswell, New Mexico, the myth has led to an entire UFO industry there. In fact the June 1997 issue of *Popular Science* quotes Roswell's mayor as saying UFOs are good for business. It also reports that community leaders are pushing the tourism industry on the back of the Roswell UFO legends.[26] As I have noted over the years, a large percentage of the UFO subculture does not seem to be about earnest people interested in the phenomenon because they have become rattled about their own UFO sightings or experiences. Frankly much of the movement is about money. There's a lot of money to be made in marketing flying saucers.

The Basic Meier Story

The gist of Meier's undocumented story is that he claims to have been selected while still a young boy as a contactee by a superior, benevolent group of extraterrestrial beings from the

135

Pleiades. In 1944 he began receiving telepathic messages from an entity known as Sfath, an old man who would appear to him periodically and whisk him up into the sky in a pear-shaped flying machine. Sfath tutored him in matters of wisdom and the universe, but he "never told me his origin and what my mission essentially was," Meier said.[27]

When Sfath's voice disappeared from his head, a new female entity named Asket, who claimed to come from an unknown parallel universe called Dal, began talking to him.[28] This voice continued for nineteen years and led him deeply into occultism and, as he put it, "greater spiritual awareness." Through listening to the voice, he became a world traveler and studied various religious philosophies. He traveled to Jerusalem, Bethlehem, Jordan, West Pakistan, India, and Turkey (where he lost his arm in a bus accident). He claims that he was retracing Jesus' footsteps by going to these places. It didn't matter to him that scholars say Jesus never went to Turkey or India; the telepathic voice of Asket said he had been there.

Meier allegedly met Semjase for the first time in 1975. Through telepathic messages she told him where she would land her beamship in the Swiss countryside, and he would go meet the landing saucer. He claims he has had numerous meetings with Semjase and other Pleiadians and that they have chosen him to help lead the world into a new age. Semjase gave Meier an alternate explanation of human history, stating that earthlings were descended from beings from Lyra (along with the Pleiadians), but that humans destroyed the planet twice during its history. To prevent that happening again, the Pleiadians want to use Meier to help guide the earth into its spiritual evolution.[29]

While under intense scrutiny from UFO investigators, Meier began claiming that his meetings with Semjase stopped in 1978, along with most of his alleged telepathic contact with aliens. In 1985 he told writer Gary Kinder that all contacts with the Pleiadians were to end in 1986 and that telepathic contact with them was greatly lessening. "At present there isn't much happening in my head," he said.[30] Nevertheless, he has remained a focal point in UFO folklore as various prominent UFO enthusiasts continue to sell his photographs along with other materials related to his alleged contacts. One group set up the Genesis III publishing group to sell Meier photographs and books, and Randolph Winters has set up a company called the Pleiadian Project that serves to teach the Meier revelations via seminars and teaching material.

Putting Emmanuel into Perspective

One of the ways the aliens hope to guide Earth's spiritual evolution is to demonstrate through Meier that Jesus Christ is not who the Bible claims he is—and to vilify the Christian church at the same time. Meier claims that Asket brought him back through time to A.D. 32, when he personally met with Jesus, whom he often refers to as Emmanuel. During the time trip, "Jesus" allegedly told Meier that Judas Iscariot was not a traitor; he was actually Christ's scribe chosen to write down the "truth" about his teachings. Judas was then instructed to bury his writings, which Meier has conveniently recovered. These writings actually make up a new bible.

"Jesus" also allegedly told Meier that he wasn't the Messiah. He knew he would be called that some day to further the religious aims of the apostle Paul. But what would be written in the Bible about him would be "deceitful lies." He also said he never died on the cross, denied his virgin birth (saying his father was actually a man trained by the Pleiadians), and denied that he was God or the Son of God.[31]

After the time travel Meier claims to know more about Jesus. And what he learned was similar to the same false gospel taught in one way or another by the UFO cultists mentioned in these pages: that Jesus didn't die on a cross; he was in a coma. Joseph of Arimathea and people from India helped nurse him back to health. As I summarized in *UFOs in the New Age:*

> Christ then moved to Damascus where he lived for two years and had a dangerous run-in with his bitter enemy, Saul of Tarsus. He then moved on to India with his mother, Mary, his brother Thomas, and Judas. There he spread his "true" teachings, and

when he was about forty-five he married a pretty Indian woman who bore him many children. He then settled in Cashmere, India, and died at age 110.[32]

Although Meier's teachings are somewhat unique in that they have helped promote the myth that at least some aliens come from the Pleiades, his revelations about Jesus are not unique. They are very similar to those of other UFO cults; they form a pattern. Notice how Meier's revelations from the Pleiadians, in a manner similar to almost all the UFO cults discussed in this book, have voided the mission of Jesus Christ, who said he came to die on the cross as a "ransom for many" (Mark 10:45). Meier's Jesus did not die on the cross. One might ask at this point: Why would aliens want to come millions of miles through space and attempt to change the way humankind think about Jesus? Voiding Christ's person, his work, and his mission seems to be of utmost importance to the gospel according to extraterrestrials.

New Doctrines

The New Testament Book of Hebrews states, "Jesus Christ is the same yesterday, today, and forever" (13:8). James the apostle tells us, "Every good and perfect gift is from above, coming down from the Father of the heavenly lights, who does not change like shifting shadows" (James 1:17 NIV). These are just two among many Bible verses that are used to argue the unchanging nature of God, which is a doctrine known as the immutability of God. Orthodox Bible scholars have always maintained that God does not change.[33] Another verse, this one from the Old Testament, states this doctrine clearly: "For I am the LORD, I do not change" (Mal. 3:6).

This doctrine is not to be confused with the doctrine of progressive revelation, which means that God revealed himself to humankind progressively, from the fall of mankind in the Garden of Eden through the time of Christ. For example, he revealed himself to Abraham and founded a nation. He then revealed himself to Moses and gave the law. Next came the prophets, and finally he revealed himself through his Son, with each step of the way building on previous revelation. I believe those who contend that God is giving us new revelations today are out of line. The Book of Hebrews tells us that Jesus Christ is the final revelation, and that in "these last days" has "spoken to us by His Son, whom He has appointed heir of all things, through whom also He made the worlds" (Heb. 1:2). True guidance from the Holy Spirit will conform to what God has revealed in his Word.

This is not true of the doctrines that allegedly come from extraterrestrials. Glaring inconsistencies and outright lies are immediately apparent in every system I have studied. The revelations allegedly given to Meier from the Pleiadians are like quicksand. They have changed dramatically, moving far away from Meier's original statements.

Since Meier had told investigators that his contacts with the Pleiadians were to end in 1986, news from Meier had been relatively sparse until 1996. It was beginning to appear that Meier had become a curiosity, the weaver of past legendary tales. But in recent days, an "Official Billy Meier Web Page" has sprung up on the Internet, claiming to be the official voice of Meier and his organization.[34] It also claims that *no one*—despite the fact that Meier's revelations from the Pleiadians have led thousands of New Age and UFO channelers to claim contact with them—could possibly be in touch with the Pleiadians, because *there aren't any!*

It states: "The Pleiades that we see in our night sky are about 420 light-years from Earth and consist of approximately 250 hot, blue stars that are still very young and incapable of sustaining life in either a course material or spiritual form." Instead, the space brothers are from the Plejaran system, which is about 500 light-years from earth, according to the Meier-linked Web site. If this is true, then why the deception? Why did Meier for years declare the Pleiades constellation as the origin point? The answer given is that putting this story out was a trick from the space brothers to expose as frauds people who were also claiming to be in contact with the Pleiadians. According to the Web page:

The truth and origin regarding the Pleiadians' real name of Plejarans was deliberately withheld from us at the Pleiadians' request

139

until February 1995, when they officially withdrew all of their bases from Earth. It was their intention to assist Billy in exposing those people fraudulently claiming to be in contact with "Pleiadians," either in a physical or spiritual form.[35]

In addition, Meier also claims that his contacts with the Pleiadians/Plejaranians have continued, contradicting previous statements that they had stopped. In fact according to the "Official Billy Meier Web Page," there have been 174 additional contacts between Meier and the Pleiadians/Plejaranians since 1978.

The Web page, which is generated from the United States, and another one from the Swiss FIGU organization have savagely attacked Meier's critics—and others formerly allied with Meier, including Randolph Winters. The Swiss Web page also attacks Meier's ex-wife.

Apparently Winters, an American, has gone beyond Meier's revelations by coming up with his own Pleiadian contactee. He is a Miami man named "Adrian" who claims to be an alleged "reborn Pleiadian living on earth." Winters (with whom I debated over the veracity of the Meier material on a Los Angeles radio station in the early 1990s[36]), the Web page declares, has produced his own fraudulent photographs of beamships. In a message allegedly put on-line by Meier, he complains that Winters stole his materials without authorization and permission and is using them to make money without bothering to send some of the cash Meier's way.[37] In an Internet message by Meier placed on the Swiss FIGU Web page, he also made similar complaints against Lee Elders, one of the principals involved with publishing Meier's photographs in America in the late 1980s and early 1990s in a two-volume set titled *Contact from the Pleiades.* He never got paid for that, Meier complained. Elders is a "thief and despicable liar," he wrote.[38]

VISIONS OF ASHTAR

In UFO circles, doctrines often form from obscure events and sometimes obscure writings and then evolve into huge building blocks for a system of beliefs. That is one of the themes of this book. One UFO enthusiast channels beings from the Pleiades, and pretty soon half the UFO community is talking about the Pleiadians. This is also the case with the "Men in Black" legend. Its roots come from a paranoid tome written by Gray Barker in 1953 called *They Knew Too Much about Flying Saucers* that alleged a government plot by mysterious men in black suits to silence those who have seen UFOs. And then there is Roswell, the obscure 1947 crash that wasn't, which has become a major pillar of UFO orthodoxy. In some UFO circles, it doesn't matter if there is a total lack of evidence for their beliefs. The myths persist—and are believed.

Sometimes these evolving myths swell up so large and take on such unbelievable dimensions that they are, well, unbelievable, and so far-fetched that they embarrass factions within the UFO community. The myths that not all ufologists are able

141

to swallow fragment, with portions of the UFO community believing one version, while other portions believe another version, and so on.

One such fragmented myth has evolved around the space brother Ashtar, who is, according to most accounts, the entity behind the Ashtar Command, a fleet of spaceships boarded by space brothers that has been locked in orbit around Earth for decades. Although the fleet is said to be run by supreme commander Ashtar, many UFO enthusiasts even say that Jesus (who is also called Sananda in UFO lore) is onboard one of the spaceships as a leading general in the Command. Others say Lucifer, or Satan, is there too. But UFO enthusiasts encourage us not to be alarmed. The devil is now a good guy helping the Ashtar Command. Members of various alien races are also aboard the Ashtar Command fleet, according to legend, but there is not full agreement as to who they are or how many ships are involved.

What is the purpose of the Ashtar Command, according to UFO mythology? Most believe they are good aliens who are here to help guide Earth to a new age. According to some versions, they will help by orchestrating a mass evacuation of worthy earthlings by beaming them up in a manner not unlike that done with *Star Trek* transporters. Later the Command will come to Earth with the earthlings to help rebuild the planet. Some versions of the Ashtar myth say there will be a mass landing of the Ashtar Command to assist Earth, but only when humankind is spiritually ready.

Many UFO contactees and New Agers have claimed to be in contact with the Ashtar Command since the early 1950s, usually through telepathy or channeling.[1] Some claim that through channeling they have touched base directly with their leader, Commander Ashtar. But in recent years controversy and infighting have developed within the UFO community over the Ashtar legend, due to new, alleged, unsavory maverick messages coming from the Ashtar Command.

It seems that a maverick general in the Ashtar Command is anti-Semitic and has pontificated exhaustive messages—even books—to earthlings from his orbiting spacecraft. Among other things the space brother alleges that Jews are evil imposters, bent on world domination, and that the Holocaust never really happened. He also asserts, even citing the writings of the ultra-right wing Lyndon LaRouche organization, that the U.S. government is involved in a worldwide conspiracy to "wipe out a good part of the global population and escape to Mars."[2]

The alleged space brother calls himself Gyeorgos Ceres Hatonn, or "Hatonn" for short. He claims to be "Commander in Chief, Earth Project Transition, Pleiades Sector Flight Command, Intergalactic Federation Fleet—Ashtar Command: Earth Representative to the Cosmic Council and Intergalactic Federation Council on Earth Transition."[3] He has pontificated on many other subjects, including the JFK assassination (he claims JFK's driver, William Greer, killed the former president). Hatonn even claims former U.S. President George Bush was involved in drug running.[4]

As one can imagine, these revelations from Hatonn have created a firestorm of controversy within ufology. Don Ecker, the publisher of the respected *UFO* magazine, angered by the fact that the alleged alien's messages were anti-Semitic and that they denied the Holocaust, ran a two-part exposé in 1992 blasting the alleged ET and his creators (the publishers of the Hatonn material, who were also the originators of the Hatonn myth), titled "A Neo-Nazi ET? 'Hatonn's World.'"[5]

In Hatonn's books, which are published by George Green of the America West Publishing Company, the space entity has even advocated that the horrifying photographs of the World War II Nazi concentration camps were fake and that the piles of thin, starved bodies released in the closing days of the war were actually dead Germans that World War II Supreme Allied Commander and future president of the United States Dwight Eisenhower allowed to starve to death! The Ashtar Command alien made some of these claims in books like *Destruction of a Planet: Zionism IS Racism* and *The Trillion Dollar Lie: The Holocaust,* volumes 1 and 2.

Just how does an alien write books? Until the arrival of Hatonn, most ET information found in books has come by way of channeling through UFO enthusiasts. This is the case with the *Urantia Book* and other volumes of revelations from space and the spirit world. What often happens in channeling (which the Bible refers to as spiritism) is that a man or woman goes into a trance that produces an altered state during which contact with spirits is made. It can take a number of forms, but the most prominent ones are automatic writing and trance channeling.[6] Hatonn, however, does things differently. This Ashtar commander claims to have sent his information on a military channel that was received and written down by the scribe, "Dharma." "Dharma is Doris Ekker, a sixty-ish grandmother who purportedly receives and then writes down the transmissions from Commander Hatonn."[7] However, on close scrutiny, Ekker the scribe turned out to be a major problem for George Green's publishing company. Some of Hatonn's messages have been found to be outright word-for-word plagiarisms of others' works. For example, in the Hatonn book *The Trillion Dollar Lie: The Holocaust,* we find the complete text of the infamous forgery, *The Protocols of the Learned Elders of Zion,* which was first presented to the Russian czar in 1903 and charged the Jews with a conspiracy to destroy society and take over the world.[8] The *Protocols* were later widely distributed by the Nazis.

Modern sources were allegedly appropriated by Hatonn as well, and among UFO enthusiasts who were offended was Swiss contactee Billy Meier. For instance, the book transmitted to "Dharma" (Doris Ekker) titled *And They Called His Name Jmmanuel* turned out to be a plagiarism of the 1984 English version of Meier's 1978 German document titled *Talmud Jmmaul.*[9] There is also the issue that Hatonn, via Ekker, reportedly plagiarized William Cooper's *Behold a Pale Horse,* which is a popular wild alien/world government conspiracy–oriented book. Reportedly following the accusations of plagiarism, Ekker was replaced as Hatonn's channel in favor of Green's wife, Desiree, who suddenly, and very conveniently, began claiming contact with Hatonn as well.

The Development of the Ashtar Myth

One of the earliest, or perhaps the earliest, individual to claim to be receiving messages from the space brother Ashtar was

George Van Tassel of Joshua Tree, California. He said that in 1952 Ashtar, claiming to belong to the Council of the Seven Lights, came to him and pledged assistance "to save mankind from himself."[10] More telepathic contacts came from Ashtar "and eventually other space brothers and sisters," and they sent Van Tassel "on a lifelong wild-goose chase of recording their words, organizing massive UFO conferences to spread the message of the benevolent space brothers," and constructing a unique building called the Integratron, which was supposed to reverse the aging process by revealing the "rest of this secret of the cross [of Jesus]."[11] The basic concept of the Ashtar Command myth—that of many flying saucers orbiting the earth ready to intervene in human history—also seems to have started with Van Tassel.

But despite raising a lot of funds for the project and despite receiving bits and pieces of channeled information on construction, Van Tassel never completed Integratron. He died suddenly in 1978. The unfinished building stands today as a monument to the "wisdom" of Ashtar and his friends. What other wisdom did Ashtar and friends allegedly give Van Tassel? They fed him lies—that Jesus was actually a ufonaut, that a future chapter of the Bible would be written about Van Tassel, that the Great Pyramid in Egypt in 1967 gave truthful information about future events and prophesied the soon destruction of modern Israel, that the beginning of the "third woe" of the Book of Revelation would begin August 20, 1967, which signified that a nuclear attack by the Soviet Union would soon take place and wipe out much of the southeastern United States.[12]

T. James, a popular contactee from the 1950s and author of the 1956 book *Spacemen: Friends and Foes,* was also associated with Van Tassel. He wrote that Ashtar possessed his body, took control of his speech, and caused him to engage in "automatic writing."[13] What were the "truths" Ashtar gave him? He affirmed that the earth is hollow and that a morally degenerate race lives at the center (a theory popular to occultists), that hoaxter George Adamski was indeed entertaining aliens, and that people allied with Satan live on the moon. Ashtar also affirmed the myth of the lost continent of Lemuria (another theme popu-

145

lar with occultists) and claimed one of their cities still existed in Antarctica from which Lemurians fly their UFOs.[14]

Ashtar Command Doctrine

The late Ruth Norman of the Unarius Society also said those associated with the Ashtar Command were lying. Her reasons were based on conflicting UFO theologies, because those proclaiming the Ashtar Command were proclaiming a different scenario of the future than hers. The Ashtar Command theology is basically the same as that of the Heaven's Gate cult. They believe the earth is going to be spaded under and that all worthy people are going to be taken aboard spacecraft during the "evacuation." As we discussed, the Unarius group believes the opposite, that the space brothers are going to come to the earth to guide it into a golden age. Doomsday has been canceled, Norman wrote.

> Do not be misled and duped by the so-called Ashtar Command and (acclaimed) 50,000 spaceships that will supposedly remove all persons from the earth while the earth will be cleansed with fire and floods and the populace meanwhile to be cleansed and resting in these spaceships located above the earth. . . . This book [by the Ashtar Command] is a very, very dangerous thing. . . . [15]

What Norman may have been talking about was a channeled book from the Ashtar Command edited by Carol Ann Rodriguez called *The New World Order: Channeled Prophecies from Space* that has continued to sell well to this day.[16] This book along with Van Tassel's and later Thelma B. Terrell's works, all claiming more contact with Ashtar, helped establish the basic premises of the Ashtar myth and the Ashtar Command. (Terrell is also known by the UFO group Guardian Action International as the channel Tuella.)

Thelma Terrell, writing as Tuella to represent her spiritual name, is a popular information source in UFO–New Age circles. Her material continues to sell. One New Age publisher has recently reprinted some of her earlier channeled material from the Ashtar Command. But this material, like almost all UFO cult material, exposes Ashtar's fallacies. In the 1982 edition of the book *Project: World Evacuation,* the Ashtar Command tells Terrell that "the early times of *this decade* will see the fulfillment of all the prophecies that have been released to the world" (emphasis mine).[17] In other words, the UFO evacuation and mass world destruction Ashtar prophesied were to have taken place in the early 1980s. How unlike a true biblical prophet!

The book boasts that it is based on thirty-five transmissions coming from a "several-miles-long" mother ship commanded by Ashtar circling the earth near the equator. According to its introduction, the messages began on July 4, 1980, when a "well-established" New York City businessman fell into a trance and his vocal cords were taken over by Ashtar.[18] It talks about how the space brothers were going to assist humankind into the new age, following great calamities on earth during which worthy earthlings would be beamed up. But it also, in keeping with other UFO literature, contradicts the Bible from cover to cover and attacks the person of Jesus Christ. In fact Ashtar is quoted in the book as declaring "Jesus does not wish to be worshipped,"[19] which is exactly the opposite of what the Bible declares (see John 20:28–29; Luke 19:37–40; Rom. 14:11; Phil. 2:9–11; Heb. 1:6; Matt. 2:2; John 9:35–38; Matt. 28:17; Rev. 4:9–11).

Over the years Ashtar Command theology has developed so much that Spiritweb, an Internet clearinghouse of UFO, occultic, and futuristic ideas, along with other Internet sites, is devoting many pages to the subject of Ashtar and his command. Spiritweb describes the cast of characters on the alleged spaceships, using the drawings of "psychic artists." The Web sites also help explain the basic theology of today's Ashtar Command. They illustrate the fact that this myth has shifted since the primitive days when Van Tassel touched base with Ashtar. First of all, the number of invisible spaceships circling planet Earth has greatly increased. In the 1980s there were thousands of them. Now there are *millions* of them.[20] And the mother ship is not just several miles long; it's one hundred miles long![21] Talk about space junk! One recent message from the Ashtar Command found on the Internet states:

The Ashtar Command is the airborne division of the Great Brother/Sisterhood of Light, under the administrative direction of Commander Ashtar and the spiritual guidance of Lord Sananda, known to Earth as Jesus, or the Christ, our Commander-in-Chief. Composed of millions of starships and personnel from many civilizations, we are here to assist Earth and humanity through the current cycle of planetary cleansing and polar realignment.[22]

But despite the talk of Jesus, or "Lord Sananda," guiding the Ashtar Command along with Ashtar, the documents quickly cut away at Jesus' uniqueness and his role as the Messiah. Instead "The Messiah" becomes a collective term, rather than the term for the Jewish Messiah. "A major focus at this time is the activation of the *collective Messiah,* the 144,000 <u>ascended masters</u>," according to a document called "The Ashtar Command: Our Mission, Purpose and Directive" (emphasis is mine, underlining is in original).[23] Who then is Jesus? He is on the same level as Moses and Elijah; in fact this is the Ashtar doctrine of the trinity (Jesus, Moses, and Elijah), which does violence to the historic Christian doctrine of the Trinity—Father, Son, and Holy Spirit. The Ashtar Command statement also recognizes Sai Baba, a discredited charlatan and madman/guru from India who claims to be God, as a "cosmic Christ."[24] It also says that Jesus is no longer "planetary christ."

Who then is the planetary christ? According to the statement, it's Lord Maitreya.

Who Is Lord Maitreya?

Benjamin Creme, a British New Age author, says that Lord Maitreya is the New Age Christ. He is the "World Teacher" who transcends all religions. He is the "Maitreya, the Buddha, the Messiah, the Imam Mahdi, or the Christ," he asserts.[25] This individual arrived in a "self-created body" in 1977, Creme has asserted, and has been living in the Asian-Indian community in the east end of London.

In 1982 Creme's organization, the Tara Center of Los Angeles, paid two hundred thousand dollars to place ads in newspapers worldwide proclaiming, "THE CHRIST IS NOW HERE." Creme followed the advertisement with declarations that Maitreya would appear before the end of the spring. This created a stir as some authors believed it and began claiming that the Antichrist of the Bible was about to be revealed.[26]

Obviously it never happened, yet Creme has continued to teach that Maitreya is now here and has produced photographs of him and accounts of his alleged miracles—none of which have been remotely verified. In fact there is evidence Creme has had to backpedal a few times with his pronouncements and claimed miracles.

Most germane to our discussion, though, is the source of Creme's information about a New Age Christ arriving at the close of the millennium. The "space people," he says. Since 1958 he has been a contactee receiving "telepathic dictation" from aliens who have made him part of their plan[27] to reveal their messiah and to bring to earth a new world order. He became interested in flying saucers in 1953 after becoming involved in the teachings of Theosophy and other related occult teachings,[28] and that progressed until Creme, by his own admission, "entered into the closest contact with, and work for, the Space Brothers."[29]

The Evacuation and Ascension

Ashtar, as channeled by Eric Klein and presented on Spiritweb, says that the invisible spaceships circling earth have been busy over the years. (If they were there since 1952, that means they have been in orbit for at least forty-five years!) They have been working to prevent earthquakes. Now, however, they are "awaiting your evacuation and ascension." In this statement there is no mention of just 144,000 who will be beamed up. Ashtar explains: "You will be taken to a ship. You will be lifted physically as an etheric and physical being. . . . All must be lifted or leave this planet in some way in the remaining years in order to make way for the Earth's clearing. . . . You will be taken to one of the mother ships. There we will have a great celebration."[30]

After the earth is spaded under, those who had been taken aboard the spaceships will be given a chance to come back "as ascended beings and to recolonize the Earth." They will also have, at that future point, godlike powers and will be like gods. Incredibly they will come back with more power than Jesus had two thousand years ago. They will

> walk side by side with humans to create quite a ruckus with your manifestations, your miracles, your ability to materialize and dematerialize at will, your ability to create out of etheric substance all that you require. I think you have heard of the powers of Sananda when he was here as Jesus. . . . you will do what He did and more.[31]

Ashtar's statement goes on to promise eternal life for those who return, for in the new world "you will be immortal and ever youthful."[32] Incredibly, some things have not changed since the Garden of Eden. People are still falling for the same lies Satan tempted Eve with—to not die, to have secret knowledge, and to be as gods (Genesis 3).

A LITANY OF LIES AND OTHER DECEPTIONS

The public is getting fed up with cults of death. Following the deaths of thirty-nine Heaven's Gate members, there were two related suicides, which further shocked our sensibilities.[1] It seems that every so often since the late 1970s, when Jim Jones ordered the mass suicide of the People's Temple, there has been increased cult violence. Although people are upset about this, it doesn't seem to have given the public a better understanding of the spiritual deception and mind control that lie at the base of cult beliefs.[2]

In the wake of the Rancho Santa Fe suicides I have granted many interviews to reporters who wanted to know what I thought of them. In each case, I outlined the spiritual element that accompanies cults of death. As I have outlined in this book, I believe many cult leaders are demonized. Through occult involvement and sometimes through a deliberate, willful act, they reject the true God, and therefore God has allowed them to follow lies. They are spiritually deceived.

This is sometimes joined with mind control, which happens over the long haul to cult members, often through a regimented diet, a lack of proper rest, and a steady stream of cult doctrine. These influences, coupled with the insular nature of cults—not allowing outside influences to filter through to the group—begin to greatly impact members' minds, and in extreme cases even take over their rational thought.

I believe there is an evil intelligence behind cults (including UFO cults), the New Age movement, and much of what we call modern spirituality. However, I have found that many people are not willing to accept that there is a definite demonic agenda behind many contemporary religious strands. I believe that one of the biggest deceptions of all is the inability to discern the intelligence behind evil. I have shown that there is an intelligent evil behind the UFO cults that also permeates New Age occultism. It is most concerned with blocking what God has said in his Word and voiding what the true Christ did on the cross two thousand years ago. This intelligence also wants to cause as much human heartache as possible in an ultimate plan to bring the world to ruin, thus destroying what God has called good. The intelligence is hard at work with the leaders of many UFO cults. They have, one by one, declared themselves to be Jesus Christ or at least his most trusted advisor. They are giving us a picture of Jesus that is, pardon the pun, alien to the Scriptures.

UFO cults and the current obsession with the unseen and the realm of space are not of God. They are evil and demonic in every language and in every culture. The obsession with space by millions who follow these false religions has led to the deaths of many today and countless others throughout the centuries who have followed primitive space-age obsessions in a myriad of cultures and settings.

I also believe the current space-age mythology may be part of a great delusion prophesied in the Bible, a deception that would sweep many people away just before the time of the return of Christ. Although Jesus said that no one knows the day or the hour of his coming, we could be close to that great event!

Another purpose behind cult delusion is to discredit Christianity and to discredit legitimate spirituality. In the mind of some people strong belief in anything spiritual is cultic, and they use incidents like the Aum Supreme Truth murders and the Solar

Temple and Heaven's Gate suicides as "proof" of what can happen if anyone believes too strongly in anything religious. For example, in the wake of the suicides, I was on a live call-in radio show in Denver discussing Heaven's Gate and UFO cults when a man called in pontificating that the reason for the deaths was a belief in religion, because that's where it leads, and there was no difference between Heaven's Gate beliefs and my brand of Christianity anyway. It would have been easy for me to shake this off as a strange minority viewpoint had we not received several other calls agreeing with the man. To some people, belief in anything supernatural is dangerous.

That is part of the reason I've talked about so many false christs in these pages. The nondiscerning person, who does not know the true historical Jesus—the true Christ—can hear about any number of false christs that can further cloud his understanding. I have had to face this with much sadness since the Heaven's Gate suicides.

I have also tried to show another dangerous aspect of UFO beliefs that doesn't have much to do with the spiritual world. That is that flying saucers are big business, and because of this the UFO subculture has become a place where con men (and women) are preying, like vultures, to separate people from their wallets. The Roswell UFO industry is a prime example of such merchandising. Some lie. Some cheat and steal. A number plagiarize. They do anything, even to the point of weaving elaborate stories about their background, educational credentials, and alleged experiences with aliens to receive attention and profit.

Some UFO conventions I have attended convincingly illustrate this point. Often UFO "experts" are also UFO salesmen and they make a great deal of money selling their UFO–related wares at their display tables. One of them, "Dr." Fred Bell, who claims he is in touch with the beautiful, blonde Pleiadian woman, Semjase, that Billy Meier was in contact with, will be happy to sell you a wire pyramid hat for more than one hundred dollars, claiming that it will give you special psychic powers. People were eagerly buying them at one UFO convention I attended. There are some folks, many of them who are not religious in orientation, who are putting these hucksters to the test—

and exposing them for the liars and financial deceivers they are. Many contactees could not successfully pass the application stage of a UFO better business bureau. My sympathies are with anyone, religious or not, who is exposing their schemes.

Truth

Those who would use the highly publicized acts of deluded cult members as an excuse for not believing in anything spiritual are themselves deceived. Spiritual principles are worth believing in if they are true. I have found that this statement is true: "For God so loved the world that He gave His only begotten Son, that whoever believes in Him should not perish but have everlasting life" (John 3:16). This is the truth that UFO cults want to deny. I have also found that UFO cult beliefs, and almost all beliefs from UFO enthusiasts involving alleged aliens, psychic contacts, abductions, bizarre UFO–government conspiracies (including Roswell and Area 51), and a host of other UFO beliefs are simply myths; they are built on shifting sand, and when the storm comes, there will be nothing left. Some of these systems are built on a foundation of a litany of lies.

The truth of God's Word, however, has stood the test of time and it has stood up to scientific and historical evaluation. Jesus Christ stands at the focal point of human history. He also stands at the crossroads of lives, patiently asking for a decision. Most, like those caught in the web of UFO cult deception, choose the broad way that leads to death.

Some people would argue that there are similarities between the Heaven's Gate cult and Christianity. Both groups believe in a better world following death. I would say, however, that there are significant differences. In an editorial in *Christianity Today,* Dean Nelson discusses this very thing. "Our purpose as Christians is not to flee this life, but to love God and others," he wrote. "Even when Heaven's Gate people were here, they fled to their own enclave. Christians do not confine their love to their own circle." He also writes that in contrast with the Heaven's Gate cult:

154

Christianity can live with ambiguity, uncertainty, critical thought, and reason. Christians don't always embrace ambiguity and criticism, but they know they have to live with them. Weak faiths are threatened by questions. Christianity is strengthened by them.

. . . The biggest difference I can see is that Heaven's Gate followers felt they needed to leave this life to go to God. My experience has shown me that God comes to us. On that first Easter morning, Jesus didn't call to Mary Magdalene from heaven. Jesus stood next to her at the empty tomb. And he called her by her name. Here.[3]

A Call for Discernment

I believe people today need discernment. Many UFO cults are out there, along with all types of other cults, including blatant counterfeits of Christianity. Therefore, people need to equip themselves so they won't be fooled. They need to put things to the test. They need to be on the lookout for inconsistencies and lies in the testimonies of their leaders, even their purported Christian leaders. They need also to be concerned with doctrine, pure doctrine, no matter which so-called "wave of the Spirit" is breezing through. Many of these waves today that are being eagerly gobbled up in churches around the world, I believe, are false.

The Bible clearly teaches that just prior to the return of Jesus, religious deception will multiply, with many religious leaders even making the claim that they are Christ (Matt. 24:24). Paul warns about "doctrines of demons" coming into the world during a future time period. He also says in 2 Thessalonians that there will be a great "falling away" just before the return of Christ and that there will be an increased "working of Satan, with all power, signs, and lying wonders" during this time period (2 Thess. 2:3, 9).

What should have gotten the people's attention when The Two, Applewhite and Nettles, crisscrossed America in 1975 recruiting followers? They should have been suspicious because of the false teachings and the inconsistent and dishonest living. I believe those with discernment would have been able to spot the fruits of the ministry that eventually resulted in death. Jesus said in Matthew 7:15–19: "Beware of false prophets, who come to you in sheep's clothing, but inwardly they are ravenous wolves. You will know them by their fruits. Do men gather grapes from thornbushes or figs from thistles? Even so, every good tree bears good fruit. . . . Every tree that does not bear good fruit is cut down and thrown into the fire."

What was the fruit of the cult as it was starting more than two decades ago? It was visibly bad, as was the background of The Two. Press reports indicate that both Nettles and Applewhite were deeply involved in the occult, while Applewhite was scandalized for sexual indiscretions that included homosexuality.

Hostile to Christianity

One story largely untold in the secular media concerning the Heaven's Gate cult is that they were not even remotely Christian (despite their use of words like *Christ, heaven,* and *the Father*) and that many of them had an extreme hatred of Christianity. This was abundantly clear from the exit statements and videotaped messages most cult members gave. These were astounding. It was as though they were shaking their fists at God on their way out. Truly we live in a post-Christian era, as the late Dr. Francis Schaeffer put it. The Heaven's Gate cultists thought they were going to a flying saucer, to a place where the historical Jesus Christ was not relevant, because they thought their leader, Marshall Applewhite, was Jesus.

How different this is from Mark Twain's fictions about comets. In "A Curious Pleasure Excursion" Twain wrote that the comet would be stopping at a number of planets, and because of that "we shall take with us, free of charge, a great force of missionaries, and shed the true light upon all the celestial orbs which, physically aglow, are yet morally in darkness. Sunday-schools will be established wherever practicable."[4]

In "Extract from Captain Stormfield's Visit to Heaven" (1907), the dead captain who is floating through space gets veered off course by a comet and winds up in heaven. Once there he is trying to describe to the head clerk of heaven's gate that he comes from earth. At first the keeper never heard of earth, since there were so few people from it that actually made it to eternity. Exasperated, Stormfield uses Jesus' name as a calling card to try to tell the clerk where he is from.

> "But you may know it from this—it's the one [planet] the Saviour saved."
> He bent his head at the Name. Then he says, gently—
> "The worlds He has saved are like to the gates of heaven in number—none can count them. What astronomical system is your world in?—perhaps that may assist."[5]

In contrast, the Heaven's Gate cult did not reverence Christ as savior. His sacrificial death on the cross was meaningless to them.

Even after the Heaven's Gate cultists took their lives, others defended their choice as *the right one,* despite the fact that they were following lies from a demented leader and there was no spaceship following the comet. Among the victims was Thomas A. Nichols, 59, the brother of actress Nichelle Nichols, who played Lieutenant Uhura on the original *Star Trek* television series. She was quick to defend her brother on the April 4, 1997, *Larry King Live* television broadcast on CNN and to vilify those who called Heaven's Gate a cult.

"I respect him as an intelligent human being who sought answers, found answers that satisfied him, and followed his heart," she said. "My brother was not duped by some charismatic devil or personage. He took twenty-one years to decide where he wanted to be and what he wanted to do."

There was even a sincere essay placed on the World Wide Web that "honored" the Heaven's Gate people for their wise choice and "brilliant" mission. "These people came to perform a mission, and completed it brilliantly," it says. "I honor you, people of Heaven's Gate, and I wish you well on your journey through the stars."[6]

God's Message from Beyond the Stars

God's message to humanity, however, was not channeled by voices from the unknown. It was spoken by the prophets. When God said something would happen, it did. When God said judgment was coming, it came. When he said he was sending his Son, Jesus arrived. When he said he loves the world, he demonstrated it. When he comes into our lives, we have a new supernatural love for each other that truly makes a difference.

Recently I was at a pastors' conference listening to Mike Mac-Intosh, pastor of the Horizon Christian Fellowship in San Diego. Mike was encouraging us to let the love of Christ for others so surround us and fill us that we can see each other as God sees us—as his very own children. Remember, he said, when you look at others, realize that God designed each one to be someone's precious child. We need to look at everyone with love and compassion. We are all children of God. This hit home to me, knowing how much I love my own three young children.

This is the type of love the UFO cults and the New Age Movement know nothing about. It is also the type of love that has for centuries spawned Christian schools and universities, hospitals, homeless shelters, hospices, relief organizations, nursing homes, and missionaries. It has gotten drug dealers off the streets and enlisted in service to help their fellow man. It has caused prostitutes to stop turning tricks. It has helped many to give up a life of sensual pleasure and greed for a life of sacrifice to God and their fellowman. God's love is the type of love that convinces a child not to lie when convenient, in the same way adults are constrained not to cheat or lie. "The love of Christ constrains us," the apostle Paul said (2 Cor. 5:14). The cults, on the other hand, do very little except try to make their cult grow, sometimes at the expense of others. They have shown little interest in becoming the "salt and light" of the earth, as Jesus said his followers would be.

It is true that many wrongs throughout history have been done by the "church" in the name of Christ. The Crusades, the Inquisition, and other wrongdoing are indefensible. But they were

158

not sanctioned by God. In those times, just as today, deceivers have entered the church and have done some ungodly things.

Other New Age Deceptions

This book is not a comprehensive listing of all the space-oriented cults operating today. Indeed there are many more out there than I have discussed, and I believe some of them are capable of having serious worldwide impact, just as Aum Supreme Truth, the Solar Temple, and Heaven's Gate have.

Unfortunately in this book I have been able to only scratch the surface to reveal the types of UFO and space-age deceptions that exist. There are thousands of people throughout the world who claim to be "star people" or "walk-ins." Many folks are obsessed with UFO channeling and New Age themes and claim their bodies have been invaded by beings from another world, who, like secret agents, are here to help usher in the new age for the benevolent space brothers. Isn't it possible that some of these entities claiming to be aliens are actually demons?

I also didn't explain how the flying saucer movement gained credibility, going from the ranks of fringe movements into the mainstream.[7] And I didn't have the space to explore other New Age deceptions that are closely related to UFO cults. One of them has to do with the growing pop acceptance of angels who are supposedly watching over us. There are now cults in operation run by people who claim to be angels, giving us the same basic message as the ufonauts—an altering of the person, nature, and work of Jesus Christ. Some of them, such as a woman who calls herself Solara, talk about a mass ascension of the planet into the new age. She, like many UFO cultists, is looking for 144,000 to initiate and talks about the planet crossing various gates to enter the new age. She and other like-minded believers come from the stars.

Yes, I believe in angels, but the image Hollywood and the New Agers have given us of them does not reflect their reality and purpose. It doesn't take long for one reading UFO literature, for example, to find out that in addition to having contact with aliens, many claim contact with angels as well. This is the same type of deception UFO contactees are involved in, and the Bible calls trafficking with any type of entity or familiar spirit witchcraft, sorcery, and spiritism. The Bible also tells us that Satan can sometimes appear as an "angel of light" (2 Cor. 11:14). I believe the delusion over near death experiences (NDEs) is another closely related deception in these last days.

Perhaps the biggest related delusion of all not covered in these pages is the ancient astronaut lies that continue to spew forth through the writings of Zecharia Sitchin, Erich von Daniken, and others. These are the writings, believed outright by many UFO cultists and increasingly by the gullible public, that the Bible is only giving us part of the true story of the human race. They say that superior aliens from other worlds—not God—seeded the earth with people. Some of them declare that Jesus was an alien who didn't die on the cross. They have once again found a way to alter his person, nature, and work.

And there is the growing interest in alleged alien abductions, which is a deception in its own right. I don't fully know what to make of some of these stories, but my research indicates that an intense involvement with the occult is almost always a prerequisite to alleged alien abduction experiences. Why is it that Bible-believing Christians are not abducted and taken aboard saucers? There may also be other, darker answers to the abduction mystery, some of which may be related to the dark times that I believe may be upon us.[8]

Are UFOs Real?

I believe UFOs are real, but they represent a demonic delusion from the other side. I also believe that some of the flying vehicles they allegedly arrive in may be the work of fallen angels; they are not physical but they are very real. In the early days of UFO research people would argue about whether UFOs are real. Today most researchers agree that they are real. But my acknowledging their reality does not mean that they are physical machines from other worlds manufactured like cars in assembly lines in Detroit. There is precious little evidence—some say no evidence—that they are physical machines. They tend to not show up on the radar screen.

Lest this sounds strange to you, let me assure you that many UFO researchers, including some that are not professing Christians, have come to the same conclusion—that UFOs are non-physical phenomena that appear to some people. This is called the "interdimensional" or "multidimensional school." John Keel, Jacques Vallee, and the grandfather of ufology, the late Dr. Allen Hynek, who created the designations for cataloguing sightings today (close encounters of the first, second, third, and fourth kind), are in this school. Keel has said in his book, *UFOs: Operation Trojan Horse,* that UFOs are related to the realm of demons. He says the demonic forces behind this deception have a Trojan horselike agenda they want to unleash on humankind.[9]

Vallee, arguably the most famous UFO researcher in the world, warns that UFO forces are dangerous and have been traced to deaths worldwide. His writings also indicated, from a secular perspective, much of what I have discovered: that ufonauts are most concerned with moving the planet's religious and social structure away from Judeo-Christian beliefs and into occultism. If UFOs are machines, and he doesn't think they are, they are somehow related to the realm of the supernatural. Vallee adds:

UFOs are real. They are an application of psychotronic technology; that is, they are physical devices used to affect human consciousness. They may not be from outer space; they may, in fact, be terrestrial-based manipulating devices. Their purpose may be to achieve social changes on this planet.[10]

In writing together about UFOs, Hynek and Vallee say:

If UFOs are indeed somebody else's "nuts and bolts hardware," then we must still explain how such tangible hardware can change shape before our eyes, vanish in a Cheshire cat manner (not even leaving a grin), seemingly melt away in front of us, or

161

apparently "materialize" mysteriously before us without apparent detection by persons nearby or in neighboring towns.[11]

Still, Vallee and others have written, the partial answer of what the alleged aliens and UFOs are may be found in folklore and anthropology, specifically in the realm of fairy tales. As Vallee wrote in his book *Passport to Magnonia:* ". . . the modern, global belief in flying saucers and their occupants is identical to an earlier belief in the fairy-faith. The entities described as the pilots of the craft are indistinguishable from the elves, sylphs, and *lutins* of the Middle Ages."[12]

According to this theory, which I believe to be very credible, today's little grey aliens ARE yesterday's fairies dancing in meadows. The difference between today and centuries past, however, is that our ancestors *knew* what those little people were—they were demons, operating in the realm of Satan. Today, since they wear jumpsuits and claim to come from spaceships, many people are willing to believe them, even though they are alleged to have performed heinous experiments and sometimes sexual acts on people.

I believe UFOs and aliens are real in a spiritual sense; they are from a dimension beyond our senses and capability to fully understand. They are part of the realm of shadows and represent an incredible delusion to humanity as we enter the new millennium. Heaven is also real, Paul said after he was brought there. But it was "inexpressible" (2 Cor. 12:4). The world of demons and seducing spirits is real.

This doesn't mean that I don't believe there is life elsewhere in the universe. We can't even determine the size of the universe, much less pretend to know its secrets. God knows the answer to this, and some day I believe he will reveal it to us. But I reject the theory of evolution, which some people believe shows that we are not alone in the universe. Their theory assumes that the conditions are probably right for other Earthlike planets to exist elsewhere; therefore intelligent life may have evolved on them as well.

UFO and space-age cults flourish because of humanity's obsession with knowing what is just ahead of us. Many people today are not optimistic about the future. Like some of the cults, they see destruction ahead and they want to be in a better place when the times turn darker. Most groups we've looked at teach, in one way or another, that the earth is about to be spaded under and they see a space-age way of escaping—through flying saucers.

To be pessimistic today is not unreasonable. Consider what has happened in this century: two world wars, vast nuclear arsenals around the globe, the proliferation of terrorism, the arrival of AIDS and other life-threatening maladies, the starvation of millions, poison gas attacks, frightening dictators, and other atrocities. It is not unreasonable to conclude the end may be closer than we think. Does anyone doubt what Hitler would have done if he had had nuclear weapons? I shudder to think what Asahara might have done with just one bomb. Millions could have died in several minutes.

The Bible talks extensively about the apocalypse. It discusses unspeakable terrors that someday will come on the planet. It strongly implies that these things will take place in a time period when Israel is a nation. Could we be living in the shadow of the apocalypse?

This future time period has been designated as the time of "Jacob's trouble," a time so bad that it will require the true Messiah's intervention (see Jer. 30:7). "Unless those days were shortened," Jesus said, talking about that future time period, "no flesh would be saved." But for those who are his, those days will be shortened, he said (Matt. 24:22). The apostle Peter talks about a future day when all the earth will melt with a "fervent heat" (2 Peter 3:10–12). The Bible also talks about the future positives, the coming of a new heaven and a new earth, and it talks about the New Jerusalem coming down from heaven to earth (Rev. 21:1–2).

So in a sense these space-driven visions of apocalypse are a counterfeit of the real thing. There *will* be an end someday. But salvation aboard UFOs is a counterfeit of true salvation. The Bible says that Jesus will come with his angels from the sky to save the world and to judge the world. There will be no more deception on that day, for "the dragon, that serpent of old, who is the Devil and Satan," who has deceived the nations for thousands of years will at first be bound (Rev. 20:2–3) then later thrown into the lake of fire (v. 10) where the future Antichrist and false prophet will also be. I believe other antichrists, the type discussed in this book, will also be there, for they have done their part in deceiving the nations in what may turn out to be one of the biggest delusions ever unleashed against humankind.

So is destruction coming? Yes, but we don't know when—or how. God can withhold his judgment to the beginning of the third millennium if he wants—or even further into the future. But let's not worry about it. The true Messiah of the world, the true Christ, has promised that he will always be with us, "even to the end of the age" (Matt. 28:20). We should be busy people, folks concerned with bringing truth, clarity, and hope to a dying world at the dawn of a new millennium. We should guard our precious time carefully, not being concerned with wild tales of conspiracy and space-age intrigues.

We must fulfill our missions with the same attitude as Christ did, because our time here, as opposed to living with Christ in eternity, is limited. "I must work the works of Him who sent Me while it is day," Jesus, the true Messiah, said. "The night is coming when no one can work. As long as I am in the world, I am the light of the world" (John 9:4–5).

PROPHECIES CONCERNING CHRIST'S FIRST COMING

Bible prophecy is true. God is a God of history and One who fulfills prophecy. As I wrote in *Soothsayers of the Second Advent,* the coming of Jesus Christ, his life, and his mission fulfilled many biblical prophecies.

Consider a few of the prophecies Christ fulfilled in his coming:

Genesis 3:15: In the Garden of Eden, God told Adam and Eve that in the future the seed of a woman would bruise Satan's head.

1 Chronicles 17:12–14 (NIV): The prophet Nathan predicted someone from King David's line would become God's Promised One: "I will establish his throne forever. I will be his father, and he will be my son. I will never take my love away from him. . . . I will set him over my house and my kingdom forever; his throne will be established forever."

Luke 1:27: He was a descendant of David, according to his mother's lineage.

Matthew 1:6, 16: He was descended from David on the side of his earthly father.

165

Deuteronomy 18:18–19: He would be like Moses, and God would require everyone to listen to his words.

Micah 5:2: He would be born in Bethlehem.

Isaiah 7:14: He would be born of a virgin.

Isaiah 35:4–6: He would open the eyes of the blind and heal the deaf, dumb, and lame.

Zechariah 9:9: He would come into Jerusalem on a donkey.

Psalm 41:9; Zechariah 11:12: He would be betrayed for thirty pieces of silver.

Isaiah 53; Psalm 22: He would be beaten and killed.

Zechariah 12:10: He would be pierced.

Psalm 22:18: Some would gamble for his garments.

Numbers 9:12: Not a bone of his body would be broken. This verse refers to the Passover lamb. Jesus was *our* Passover Lamb. John called him the Lamb of God (John 1:29).

Isaiah 53:9: He would be buried in the grave of a rich man.

Psalm 16:9–10; 21:4: He would be resurrected.

On the basis of this, can we say that God would be any less specific about his prophecies concerning the last days?

APPENDIX

QUESTIONS AND ANSWERS

Q: Many contemporary UFO cults and New Age groups achieve contact with spirits through channeling. What can possibly be wrong with that? It doesn't seem to hurt anyone.

A: Let's look at some of the Bible's warnings against channeling. The prophet Isaiah, writing about 2,700 years ago, gave this word from the Lord: "And when they say to you, 'Seek those who are mediums and wizards, who whisper and mutter,' should not a people seek their God? Should they seek the dead on behalf of the living?" (Isa. 8:19).

The passage then goes on to say that there is no light in them and that they will fall under judgment—even to the point of being "driven into darkness" (vv. 20–22). In Exodus 22:18 God tells Moses that he should not allow a witch to live. Leviticus 19:31 says this: "Give no regard to mediums and familiar spirits; do not seek after them, to be defiled by them: I am the LORD your God." In the next chapter God states that he will cut off from his people the person who practices spiritism (20:6). Deuteronomy 18:10–12 is also stern: "There shall not be found among you anyone who . . . practices witchcraft . . . or a medium, or a spiritist."

King Saul was judged by God because he tried to consult with the spirit of Samuel, who was dead, and that was the reason he lost his crown and suffered a wretched death. In that case Saul consulted with a witch who agreed to try to bring up the spirit of Samuel to bring him advice. But instead of the witch bringing up a familiar spirit *to pose as Samuel,* God, in judgment, allowed the *real* Samuel to come back and pronounce God's wrath on Saul. Even the witch was terrified to see the real spirit of Samuel arrive on the scene. "So Saul died . . . because he consulted a medium for guidance," the Bible says in 1 Chronicles 10:13, summarizing the story.

In the New Testament more of the powers behind the scene that are detailed as sorcerers and mediums are placed under judgment through the power of God. The early church is launched with signs and wonders. Paul struck Elymas the sorcerer blind in Acts 13:6–12. In Acts 16:16–18, Paul casts a demon out of a medium/channeler that had given her the power to have communication with familiar spirits. Later in 1 Timothy, Paul links so-called revelations from spirits directly with doctrines of demons (4:1) and states that in the latter times "some will depart from the faith, giving heed to" these "deceiving spirits." In 2 Corinthians, Paul tells us that Satan is capable of transforming himself into an angel of light (11:14). This is especially interesting in light of the fact that nearly every NDEr reports meeting a being of light.

So although talk shows are abuzz with channelers going into trances and bringing messages from the other side into living rooms on a daily basis, and although printed messages from the other side—such as the *Urantia Book* (a book that was allegedly channeled by "supermortal beings" from space), *A Course in Miracles,* and *The Celestine Prophecy*—are the rage today, these practices are so serious to God that they can affect one's eternal destiny. The apostle Paul, writing in the Book of Galatians, tells us that those who practice the works of the flesh "will not inherit the kingdom of God" (5:21). One of the works that he lists is witchcraft. The apostle John, who was shown a heavenly vision, tells us that the "fearful, and unbelieving, and the abominable, and murderers, and whoremongers, *and sorcerers,* and idolaters, and all liars, shall have their part in the lake which burneth with fire and brimstone: which is the second death" (Rev. 21:8, emphasis mine).

Q: You mentioned in this book that both Applewhite and Nettles, the founders of what became the Heaven's Gate cult, abandoned their original families, children and all, when they began their cult. Is there anything new to report on this?

A: Yes, Mark Applewhite, the forty-year-old son of the dead cult leader, is a Christian who works at the Annapolis Christian Church in Corpus Christi, Texas, and he used the opportunity of the Heaven's Gate deaths to testify of Christ. He told the Associated Press that his family are real Christians "with the real ticket to heaven."

"I am appalled by the things that have resulted from the actions of my father and others in that cult," the younger Applewhite said.

It is also true that a daughter of Nettles is an evangelical Christian and is married to a pastor in the Calvary Chapel movement.

Q: It appears as if Nettles, one of the founders of the Heaven's Gate cult, was at one time deeply into astrology. You also wrote that astrology was one of the foundations of the murderous Solar Temple cult. What is so bad about this practice, if anything?

A: True, both Nettles and the Solar Temple group were into astrology. I also pointed out that the ancient Baal worship system was also based on astrology. Many other UFO cults are into this form of occultism, as are many New Age adherents. But the Bible resoundingly condemns astrology and in its condemnation says that astrology is akin to spiritism.

Jouret, of the Solar Temple, taught that people need to be burned up as by the sun to be purified. The truth is that people who repent of their sins and believe in the *Son of God,* Jesus, are *cleansed of their sins* and will spend an eternity with God after a time of service to him on Earth.

The Bible says we can have an assurance of salvation and eternal life. The apostle John wrote:

> He who has the Son has life; he who does not have the Son of God does not have life. These things I have written to you who believe in the name of the Son of God, that you *may know that you have eternal life,* and that you may continue to believe in the name of the Son of God.
>
> 1 John 5:12–13 (emphasis mine)

The Bible also says that if we believe, nothing can separate us from the love of God: "Neither death nor life, nor angels nor principalities nor powers, nor things present nor things to come, nor height nor depth, nor any other created thing, shall be able to separate us from the love of God which is in Christ Jesus our Lord" (Rom. 8:38–39).

God says the counsel of astrologers is worthless and won't even save the astrologers, and those who worship and serve the hosts of heaven will similarly fall under God's judgment (see Deut. 4:19; 17:1–5; 18:9–11; 2 Kings 17:16–17; 23:5; Isaiah 47:13–14; Jer. 8:2; 19:13; Ezek. 8:16; Amos 5:26–27). John Ankerberg and John Weldon point out: "The

169

Bible teaches that astrology is not only a futile (worthless) activity, but an activity so bad that its very presence indicates God's judgment has already occurred" (Acts 7:42–43).[1]

Q: Why do so many UFO cults talk about the Bible and use Christian terminology while their doctrines and practices seem to be anti-Christian? Why do so many leaders of these cults talk about Christ or actually claim to be Christ?

A: Don't be confused by the talk about Jesus and the Christian Scriptures that is so much a part of UFO literature. UFO cults, which are fundamentally New Age, quasi-Hinduistic groups, are *hostile* toward orthodox Christianity and the Jesus of the Bible. As I forcefully pointed out in *UFOs in the New Age,* the "Jesus" of the UFO cults and the New Age is a counterfeit; he is not the Jesus of the Bible. The Bible talks about many in the last days coming to bring deception to the world, claiming to be Jesus. Paul warned against people accepting a different Jesus (2 Cor. 11:3–4), or a different gospel (Gal. 1:6). The UFO cults redefine Jesus in various ways, taking something away from his person, nature, or work.

The UFO and New Age jesuses are evil imposters, doomed to perdition. The real Jesus is God in human flesh, the second person of the Trinity, who died for the sins of the world and rose again the third day just outside Jerusalem. He is also the prophesied Jewish Messiah, the one who fulfilled numerous prophecies, right on down to his birthplace, his genealogy, and the fact that he would enter Jerusalem on a donkey. None of the self-proclaimed jesuses mentioned in recent years, whether they come from Texas (Applewhite), Waco (Koresh), Guyana (Jim Jones), Korea (The Rev. Sun Myung Moon), Montana (Elizabeth Claire Prophet), France (Rael), Georgia (York), Switzerland, Japan, and dozens of other locations, fit the biblical criteria.

Another evil, unbiblical misrepresentation of Jesus, contained in numerous messages from New Age and UFO cults, is that the second coming of Christ is when a christ spirit will come and diffuse the entire planet. Some ideas like this stem from Blavatsky and later from Rudolf Steiner, who founded the Anthroposophy Society.[2]

The concept of "Christ" is linked to the Jewish Messiah—one person. He is not a force. He is not a "collective Messiah" as some UFO cults proclaim. He is one person for all time who was uniquely God and human. He is the Word who became flesh in Mary's womb at conception nine months before his birth in a Bethlehem manger. Similarly, the Holy Spirit is also a personality. He is not a force as various cults teach.

Q: UFO enthusiasts say they are not anti-Christian. They are just keeping up with the times. Their material is more current than the Bible since they are receiving new revelations and sometimes new light on the Bible from aliens. Their revelations, then, are extrabiblical. What do you say about this?

A: These variant readings of the Bible and new revelations coming from ufonauts, spirits, so-called angels, and other sources in these perilous times are all typical of cultic systems. All religious cults adhere to extrabiblical revelation to sustain themselves. UFO cults are no different. But God warns in Revelation 22:18–19 that those who would take away from or add anything to "the prophecy of his book" will be cursed forever. Although this passage refers to the Book of Revelation that the apostle John wrote under the inspiration of the Holy Spirit, Deuteronomy 12:32 and Proverbs 30:6 warn us against adding anything to God's words.

Additionally, we have no need of new revelations, because we have the Scriptures, which are God-breathed (2 Tim. 3:15–17). We as Christians also have the testimony of the Holy Spirit in our hearts that guides us into all truth. Furthermore, Hebrews 1:1–2 states that God has spoken to us in these days through his Son.

Q: Do you see any relationship between UFOs, space-age obsessions, and Bible prophecy?

A: This is difficult since not all Christians are in agreement over how Bible prophecy can be interpreted. There are three major views of Bible prophecy: premillennial, postmillennial, and amillennial. There are also additional interpretations that branch off from these. But to answer this question, I can report some of what the Bible has to say about the endtimes.

It may be that UFO cults, space-age obsessions, and other destructive cults are part of the overall biblical picture given of a great worldwide delusion that will occur just before Christ returns. If this is so, we may see even more rampant deception.

The apostle Paul told his young convert Timothy that "the Spirit expressly says that in latter times some will depart from the faith, giving heed to deceiving spirits and doctrines of demons" (1 Tim. 4:1). Later in 2 Timothy he is more specific: "For the time will come when they will not endure sound doctrine, but according to their own desires, because they have itching ears, they will heap up for themselves teachers; and they will turn their ears away from the truth, and be turned aside to fables" (2 Tim. 4:3–4).

171

I personally believe that the coming of the Lord draws near, and we had better be ready for this great event! If we are nearing this time period or even now in the endtimes, we should redouble our efforts, as Paul told Timothy: "Preach the word! Be ready in season and out of season. Convince, rebuke, exhort, with all longsuffering and teaching" (2 Tim. 4:2).

But we need to be careful. There is a lot of reckless teaching today regarding Bible prophecy. The Bible teaches in Matthew 24:36 that no one knows the day or the hour of his coming. As Jesus ascended to heaven among his last words were, "It is not for you to know times or seasons which the Father has put in His own authority" (Acts 1:7). Still, having an inner hope that Jesus could come back at any time should "purify" us, and so we should live with that expectancy (see 1 John 3:1–3). That is why I shudder whenever I hear a professing Christian or anyone pooh-poohing the reality of Jesus' return. He *will* come again to save the world from destruction and to usher in his kingdom.

We need to be careful not to overreact to New Age and UFO cult predictions of a coming disaster to Earth—sometimes they call it "the cleansing"—and think that something cataclysmic won't happen to planet Earth. Satan is a great counterfeiter, and the Bible teaches (in Matthew 24; 2 Thessalonians 2; 1 Timothy 4; and other places) that deception will increase as we near the time of judgment. According to one school of Bible prophecy interpretation, the deception will culminate in a world leader coming on the scene during a time of trouble, the Antichrist, whom people will worship as God. He will lead the world to ruin. If this really is a crucial time of history leading to the second coming of Christ, then Satan also knows it and he is fashioning multiple deceptions worldwide about the endtimes that are succeeding in drawing scores of people into an eternity without Christ.

Christian author Dave Hunt, when speaking at the Human Potential Foundation conference, talked of a potential link to Bible prophecy as he spoke about the dangers of ET contact. "What we are seeing is staggering," Hunt said. "Not only spirit mediums, psychics, yogis, and kooks, but now top scientists are seriously attempting to contact 'spirit beings' whom they believe are highly evolved, godlike entities with great knowledge and more powers than humans possess. It takes little insight to realize that the attempt to contact nonphysical entities opens the door for all kinds of Satanic deception that could be used in putting Antichrist in power!

"The Bible indicates that in the midst of the terror and chaos a man will arise known as the Antichrist. . . . Whatever one believes about

UFOs and ETs, there is no reason for hope from that quarter, but only fear. There is great hope, however, in the solution the Bible offers, and nowhere else."[3]

Hunt may be right. Our society is rapidly moving away from rationalism, and into irrationalism. Many folks are ready to believe in anything that gives them hope but they won't accept the Bible. In fact according to a 1990 Gallup poll, 47 percent of Americans believe UFOs are "real," 46 percent believe intelligent life exists in outer space, 27 percent believe that UFOs have actually touched down and visited Earth, and 14 percent of Americans have seen a UFO.[4]

Q: The Solar Temple and Heaven's Gate cults didn't seem to have many concrete facts behind their decision to go to a better world following their death. What kind of facts do Christians have for their hope of eternal life?

A: We have a much more sure future ahead of us if we believe in Jesus, whose death and resurrection was one of the best supported facts of the ancient world. Because he rose from the dead, we will rise again to be with him. Paul wrote that he has given us his Holy Spirit as "a guarantee" and a testimony that "we are always confident, knowing that while we are at home in the body we are absent from the Lord" and that when we are "absent from the body" we will be "present with the Lord" (2 Cor. 5:5–6, 8).

Q: Is it possible that UFO contactees such as Eduard "Billy" Meier and others are actually in contact with the other side through channeling and telepathy? And if so, is it possible that they are in contact with demonic angels?

A: Certainly! Second Corinthians 11:14 states that Satan can sometimes disguise himself as an angel of light. I believe this is part of the nature of deception and has been so since the Garden of Eden. It is very possible that Meier received some of his "revelations" supernaturally from various entities. They could be demons posing as aliens that gave him their doctrines, which have in turn spread into the UFO community and from there throughout the world. The Bible talks about delusions in the latter times coming from the "doctrines of demons" (1 Tim. 4:1). But if this is so, I also believe that Meier and his cohorts have tried to further those deceptions through lies and photographic tricks in an attempt to extend their credibility.

173

WHERE TO GO FOR HELP

The following ministries can provide information and help on the cults and other delusions.

Eastern Christian Outreach
P.O. Box 133
Walnutport, PA 18088

Spiritual Counterfeits Project
P.O. Box 4308
Berkeley, CA 94704
http://www.scp-inc.org/

Personal Freedom Outreach
P.O. Box 26062
St. Louis, MO 63136
http://www.pfo.org/

Reasoning Through the Scriptures Ministries
P.O. Box 80087
Rancho Santa Margarita, CA 92688
http://www.home.earthlink.net/~ronrhodes

TruthQuest Institute
P.O. Box 227
Loomis, CA 95650
http://www.truthquest.org/

Watchman Fellowship
P.O. Box 13340
Arlington, TX 76094-0340
http://www.watchman.org/

INTERNET WEB SITES ON UFOs, UFO CULTS, AND RELATED SUBJECTS

There are literally thousands of Internet Web sites operating that deal in one way or another with UFOs. Please use caution when using material from some Web sites; it is not always accurate.

The following Web sites relate to the subject matter of this book.

Heaven's Gate:

- Academic Readings on Heaven's Gate, Internet site: *http://www .trancenet.org/heavensgate/*
- Internet site: *http://www.heavensgatetoo.com/*
- James S. Phelan, "Looking for the Next World," *New York Times* magazine (February 29, 1987), Internet site: *http://www.nytimes .com/library/national/mag/*. To reach archives, enter author's name to retrieve article.

Area 51:

- "Area 51: Military Facility, Social Phenomenon, and State of Mind," Internet site: *http://www.ufomind.com/area51/*

UFO Magazine:

- *http://www.ufomagazine.com*

New Mexico Mutual UFO Network:

- New Mexico Mutual UFO Network interview with remote viewer Ed Dames: *ftp://ftp.hkstar.com/.1/ufo/psi.tech/*

Spiritweb, the New Age, and UFO Information Source:

- *http://www.spiritweb.org/Spirit/our-mission-athena.html*

Alien Autopsy Exposed:

- *http://www.parascope.com/nb/abraindx.htm*

Ted Daniels and His Millennium Watch:

- *http://www.channel1.com/mpr/pbelt.html*

Solar Temple:

- Ontario Consultants on Religious Tolerance, "Solar Temple (International Chivalric Order Solar Tradition)," Internet site: *http://www .religioustolerance.org/dc_solar.htm*

Raelian Movement:

- *http://www.rael.org/*
- Glenn Campbell, "Report of Rael Press Conference in Las Vegas, 3/11/97," *Area 51 Mailing List Archive,* Internet site: *http://www .ufomind.com/area51/list.1997/mar/a12–002.shtml*

Unarius Academy of Science:

- "Unarius Academy of Science," Internet site: *http://www.teleport .com/~dkossy/unarius.html*
- See also Unarius home page at Internet site: *http://www.serve.com/ unarius/*

Malachi Z. York and the Holy Tabernacle Ministries:

- "The Many Faces of Dr. Malachi Z. York," Internet page of the Holy Tabernacle Ministries: *http://www2.gsu/edu/~phpgls/mzy.htm*
- "Our Story!" Internet document explaining the history of the Holy Tabernacle Ministries: *http://www.geocities.com/Area51/ Corridor/4978/ourstory.html*
- Malachi Z. York, "Debate One: I Am the Real Thing," Internet site: *http://www.netgenius.com/amom/debate1.htm*

George King and the Aetherius Society:

- *http://www.aetherius.org/*

Eduard "Billy" Meier and His Related FIGU Organization:

- FIGU's Web page found at Internet site: *http://web.eunet.ch:80/ figu/FIGUHP51.HTM*
- *http://www.billymeier.com*

Mark-Age, Inc.:

- *http://www3.islandnet.com/arton/markage.html*

Gabriel of Sedona:

- *http://www.sedona.net/aquarian/gabrielbio.html*

NOTES

Introduction

1. Carol Morello, "Cultists' Bodies, Words Yielding Clues," *Philadelphia Inquirer,* 29 March 1997, A1.

2. Carol Morello, "The Mind-Set of Members," *Philadelphia Inquirer,* 30 March 1997, A1.

3. "Will," who was interviewed in silhouette on the March 27 program, was not further identified, except to say he was a North Carolina man who left the cult.

Chapter 1 Riding on the Tail of a Comet

1. Samuel Langhorne Clemens, "Extract from Captain Stormfield's Visit to Heaven," *The Complete Short Stories of Mark Twain,* ed. Charles Neider (New York: Doubleday, 1957), 564–68.

2. Ibid., 571.

3. Samuel Langhorne Clemens, "A Curious Pleasure Excursion," *The Complete Humorous Sketches and Tales of Mark Twain,* ed. Charles Neider (New York: Doubleday, 1961), 245–49.

4. Twain was fascinated with comets. In 1909 he said: "I came in with Halley's Comet in 1835. It is coming again next year, and I expect to go out with it. It will be the greatest disappointment of my life if I don't go out with Halley's Comet. The Almighty has said, no doubt: 'Now here are these two unaccountable freaks; they came in together, they must go out together.' Oh, I am looking forward to that." He got his wish. He died in 1910. (David Ritchie, *Comets, the Swords of Heaven* [New York: New American Library, 1985], 26.)

5. Ibid., 21.

6. Ibid., 3.

7. Nigel Calder, *The Comet Is Coming* (London: British Broadcasting Corporation, 1980), 12–13.

8. Ritchie, *Comets, the Swords of Heaven,* 27–29.

9. Calder, *The Comet Is Coming,* 13.

10. William Alnor, *Soothsayers of the Second Advent* (Grand Rapids: Revell, 1989), 71.

11. Ibid.; interview with Frank Maloney, Villanova University, 28 March 1989.

12. Although dozens of comets are spotted every year, the ones that gain the most attention are those considered to be "star grazers." This type of comet goes near enough to stars, or in our case, the sun, for its solar winds and heat to begin to melt the comet, thereby producing a tail. The tails can differ, but generally speaking, depending on the composition of the comet and even things such as its age, the closer a comet gets to the sun in its elliptical orbit, the longer and more spectacular its tail.

13. To be sure, Kohoutek turned out to be a better-than-average comet but it didn't live up to Berg's expectations.

14. David F. Webber and Noah Hutchings, *Apocalyptic Signs in the Heavens* (Oklahoma City: Southwest Radio Church, 1979), 21–22.

15. See my discussion of this in *UFOs in the New Age* (Grand Rapids: Revell, 1992), 134–40.

16. F. Duane Lindsey, "Judges," in *The Bible Knowledge Commentary: Old Testament,* ed. John F. Walvoord and Roy Zuck (Wheaton: Scripture Press, 1985), 383.

17. Thomas L. Constable, "1 Kings," in *The Bible Knowledge Commentary,* 583.

18. "Ashtoreth," in *New International Dictionary of the Bible,* ed. Merrill C. Tenney (Grand Rapids: Zondervan, 1987), 101.

19. John D. Davis, ed., "Molech," in *Davis Dictionary of the Bible,* 4th ed. (Old Tappan, N.J.: Revell, 1977), 532.

20. *Boyd's Bible Handbook* (Eugene, Oreg.: Harvest House, 1983), 93–94. Amos 5:26 in the King James Version: "But ye have borne the tabernacle of your Molech and Chiun your images, the star of your god, which ye made to yourselves." The *New International Dictionary of the Bible,* p. 203, states that Chiun was "possibly Saturn as god, but the meaning of the Hebrew word is uncertain."

21. Brad Steiger, *The Fellowship* (New York: Ballantine, 1989), 67–68.

22. Michael Emery and Edwin Emery, *The Press and America,* 8th ed. (Needham Heights, Mass.: Allyn & Bacon, 1996), 599.

23. "Movieweb: Top 50 All-Time Highest Grossing Movies" (September 1997). Internet site: *http://movieweb.com/movie/alltime/.*

24. There are many books that discuss the evidence for the reliability of Scripture. One of the more famous ones is Josh McDowell's *Evidence That Demands a Verdict* (San Bernardino, Calif.: Campus Crusade for Christ, 1972).

Chapter 2 A Telepathic Hoax

1. Heaven's Gate, "Last Chance Statement" of 16 January 1994. Internet site: *http://www.heavensgatetoo.com/.*

2. "Last chance to evacuate earth before it's recycled," edited transcript of videotape, 29 September 1996.

3. "Undercover 'Jesus' Surfaces before Departure," January 1997 statement. Internet site: *http://www.heavensgatetoo.com/.*

4. "Academic Readings on 'Heaven's Gate.'" Internet site: *http://www.trancenet.org/heavensgate/.* This is also corroborated by other sources, including Leon Jaroff, "The Man Who Spread the Myth," *Time* (April 14, 1997). Internet site: *http://pathfinder.com/time/magazine . . . m/970414/.*

5. It would take many pages to recount the rumors floating around in UFO circles about Area 51. Many ufologists claim that the late President Harry S Truman made contact with alleged aliens at the site and established a top secret "MJ12" working group to consult with them. Others say live aliens are housed underground at the site, as well as

at another site in New Mexico. Other more sinister rumors are that the aliens have given the U.S. government flying saucer technology in exchange for a green light to abduct citizens and perform experiments. Many say they have seen strange aircraft buzzing around the base. All these theories, and many more not covered here, are unsubstantiated.

6. "Area 51: Military Facility, Social Phenomenon and State of Mind." Internet site: *http://www.ufomind.com/area 51/.*

7. "Academic Readings on 'Heaven's Gate.'"

8. Whitley Strieber, *Communion* (New York: Beech Tree, 1987); Strieber, *Transformation: The Breakthrough* (New York: Avon, 1989); Strieber, *Breakthrough* (New York: Harper, 1997).

Strieber insists in an Internet message that he never did fully support the theory. According to his posting found at *http://www.marsweb.com/~watcher/culwhit/:* "I was neutral toward it, but suggested that if the object was there, we all try meditating at the same time because the visitors seem responsive to this. Also, though, I became suspicious when Dr. Brown said that rolls of film were involved. Professional scopes do not shoot 35mm. So I released the picture he had sent me and Art—as did Art—and it was soon proved to be a fraud."

9. John Fleck, "Rumors of Aliens Trail Comet," *Albuquerque Journal,* 3 December 1996. Internet site: *http://www.abqjournal.com/news/3news12–3/.*

10. Ibid.

11. Ibid.

12. Internet site: *http://www.heavensgatetoo.com/.*

13. Chuck Shramek, "Press Release, 28 March 1997." Internet site: *http://www.neosoft.com/~cshramek/press/.*

14. Jaroff, "The Man Who Spread the Myth."

15. Ibid.

16. K. C. Cole, *Los Angeles Times,* "A Scientific Look at Hale-Bopp." Placed on the *Philadelphia Inquirer*'s "Philadelphia Online." Internet site: *http://www.phillynews.com/packages/halebopp/come30/.*

17. "Academic Readings on 'Heaven's Gate.'"

18. Ibid.

19. Debby Stark, "Talking to Ed Dames," *New Mexico Mutual UFO Network News* 6 and 7 (June and July 1993). Internet site: *ftp://ftp.hkstar.com/.1/ufo/psi.tech/.*

20. Ibid.

21. Courtney Brown, *Cosmic Voyage* (New York: Dutton, 1996).

22. Thomas Ropp, "Book Details Contact with Jesus, Extraterrestrials," *Fort Worth Star-Telegram,* 3 March 1996, p. 71.

23. Ibid.

24. William M. Alnor, *Heaven Can't Wait: A Survey of Alleged Trips to the Other Side* (Grand Rapids: Baker, 1996), 81–82.

25. Mark Albrecht and Brooks Alexander, "Thanatology," *Spiritual Counterfeits Journal* (April 1977): 6.

26. Tal Brooke, *The Other Side of Death: Does Death Seal Your Destiny?* (Wheaton: Tyndale House, 1979), 34.

27. Thomas Ropp, "Negotiating Cosmic Traffic," *Fort Worth Star-Telegram,* 3 March 1996, p. 71.

28. Ropp, "Book Details . . . Contact with Jesus," 71.

29. Ibid.

30. Ibid.

31. Timothy Ferris, "All That Glitters Is Not God," *Rolling Stone* (January 20, 1975): 45.

32. Cited in "Scholars Submit New Arguments to Shred Space 'Chariots' Theory," CARIS tract, Santa Ana, Calif.

33. Ibid.

Chapter 3 Deeper into Madness

1. Daniel LeDuc, "'Heaven's Gate' Opens in a Mental Ward," *Philadelphia Inquirer,* 30 March 1997, A1.

2. Bill Hoffman and Cathy Burke, *Heaven's Gate: Cult Suicide in San Diego* (New York: Harper, 1997), 70.

3. Ibid., 71.

4. Ibid., 95.

5. Ibid., 112.

6. Ron Rhodes, *The Counterfeit Christ of the New Age Movement* (Grand Rapids: Baker, 1990), 121.

7. See Alnor, *UFOs in the New Age,* 41, 47, 111.

8. Brad Steiger, *Gods of Aquarius* (New York: Berkeley, 1983), 134.

9. James S. Phelan, "Looking for the Next World," *New York Times* magazine (February 29, 1987). Internet site: *http://www.nytimes.com/library/national/mag/.*

10. Hoffman and Burke, *Heaven's Gate,* 130–31.

11. Wayne Wilson, "Spacecraft Sect . . . Disenchanted Fight Movement, Leaders," *Sacramento Bee,* 22 November 1975, A1.

12. "'88 Update: The UFO Two and Their Crew," a Brief Synopsis.

13. LeDuc, "'Heaven's Gate' Opens in a Mental Ward," A1.

14. Hoffman and Burke, *Heaven's Gate,* 124.

15. LeDuc, "'Heaven's Gate' Opens in a Mental Ward," A1.

16. Hoffman and Burke, *Heaven's Gate,* 129.

17. Martha Mendoza, "In N.M., Cult Left Vivid Reminders," *Philadelphia Inquirer,* 31 March 1997, A2.

18. Watchman Fellowship, *ONLINE,* "A Christian Analysis of Heaven's Gate." Internet site: *http://www.watchman.org/.*

19. In fact humans will judge the angels in heaven, according to the apostle Paul in 1 Corinthians 6:3.

20. The Bible also teaches that believing is not just giving mental assent to the fact that Jesus died for our sins. Believing in a biblical sense means acting on your belief. It does a person no good if he is standing at the foot of the Empire State Building directly under the path of an onrushing falling piano if he simply says to shouting bystanders that "he believes" their warnings that a piano may hit him. He has to act on his belief by jumping out of the way. Similarly, if we believe Jesus has died for our sins, we will act on that by repenting of our sins and saying what the apostle Paul said on the Damascus Road, "Lord, what do You want me to do?" (Acts 9:6).

Chapter 4 Endtime Delusions

1. James J. Brookes, *Maranatha or the Lord Cometh* (Saint Louis: Edward Bredell, 1878), 364.

2. Seventeenth-century Archbishop Ussher of Armagh, Ireland, calculated that the creation of the world took place on October 26, 4004 B.C., at nine o'clock in the morning. Few Bible scholars take this seriously.

3. Ralph Woodrow, *His Truth Is Marching On: Advanced Studies on Prophecy in the Light of History* (Riverside, Calif.: Ralph Woodrow Evangelistic Association, 1977), 22.

4. Steiger, *Gods of Aquarius*, 39–40.

5. Steiger, *The Fellowship*, 50.

6. Winfield S. Brownell, *UFOs: Key to Earth's Destiny!* (Lytle Creek, Calif.: Legion of Light, 1980), 78–81.

7. Ibid., 78.

8. David Spangler, *Links with Space* (Marina Del Rey, Calif.: DeVorss, 1976), 13.

9. Ibid., 28.

10. Brownell, *UFOs*, 156–57.

11. Cited in Heaven's Gate's paper, *Our Position against Suicide.*

12. Watchman Fellowship, "Profile: Church Universal and Triumphant." Internet site: *http://rampages.onramp.net/~watchman/unipro.htm.*

13. Ashtar Command, *Project: World Evacuation,* compiled by Tuella (Salt Lake City: Guardian Action International, 1982), x–xi. See also Alnor, *UFOs in the New Age,* 51–52.

14. Robb Fulcher, "Story of Spacemen Broadcast by Man," *The* (Portland) *Oregonian,* 8 May 1984, B2. See also Alnor, *UFOs in the New Age,* 50.

15. See "The Ashtar Command: Our Mission, Purpose and Directive." Internet site: *http://www.spiritweb.org/Spirit/our-mission-athena.html.*

16. Douglas Curran, *In Advance of the Landing: Folk Concepts of Outer Space* (New York: Abbeville Press, 1985), 38–39.

17. Ibid., 33.

18. Mike Granberry, "Cultists Dwell on Their Past Lives," *Akron* (Ohio) *Beacon Journal,* 3 October 1986, D3. Granberry is a staff writer for the *Los Angeles Times,* the publication that originated the story of Norman.

19. One of the largest industries in Roswell is the UFO industry. The town hosts two UFO museums, and many businesses in the community sell UFO–related memorabilia, not to mention various guided tours of at least three alleged flying saucer crash sites near the city.

20. Bruce Handy, "Roswell or Bust," *Time* (June 23, 1997): 64.

21. Various Web sites are devoted to *Star Trek* lore. One that mentions the Ferengi-Roswell episode is *http://www.holodeck3.com/d_quark.html.*

22. Leon Jaroff, "Did Aliens Really Land?" *Time* (June 23, 1997): 69–70. This article gives a good sequence, showing how the Roswell legend grew over time.

23. Ibid., 70–71.

24. Ibid., 71.

25. Fox television examined the controversy in a show titled "Alien Autopsy—Fact or Fiction." Other networks have also been looking at the controversy. One television network, using a dummy, showed how such an autopsy could have been faked. For further information see "Abra Cadaver! Alien Autopsy Exposed." Internet site: *http://www .parascope.com/nb/abraindx.htm.*

26. James J. Hurtak, "Extraterrestrial/Ultraterrestrial Paradigms for the Future" (paper presented at "When Cosmic Cultures Meet" conference, sponsored by the Human Potential Foundation, Washington, D.C., 27–29 May 1995), 55.

Chapter 5 Hitching a Ride to Sirius

1. Virginia Essene and Sheldon Nidle, *You Are Becoming a Galactic Human* (Santa Clara, Calif.: S.E.E. Publishing Company, 1994). Cited by Ted Daniels, "New Genesis, New Exodus: The Photon Belt," *Millennial Prophecy Report.* Internet site: *http://www .channel1.com/mpr/pbelt.html.*

2. Ibid.

3. Steiger, *Gods of Aquarius,* 237.

4. Robert K. Temple, *The Sirius Mystery* (New York: St. Martin's, 1976), jacket blurb.

5. At 4.3 light-years away, the Alpha Centauri system (comprised of three stars) is closest to the sun. Sirius is about 8.6 light-years from the sun.

6. Hurtak, "Extraterrestrial/Ultraterrestrial Paradigms," 50.

7. Although Crowley was to dominate this organization, Dr. Ted Daniels of the Millennial Watch Institute says he was not the original founder.

8. Ed Conroy, *Report on* Communion (New York: William Morrow, 1989), 283.

9. Alnor, *UFOs in the New Age,* 148.

10. Colin Wilson, *Aleister Crowley: The Nature of the Beast* (Wellingborough, England: Aquarian Press, 1988), 71.

11. Aleister Crowley, *The Book of the Law* (York Beach, Maine: Samuel Weiser, 1976), 7.

12. Steiger, *Gods of Aquarius,* 237.

13. Richard Lacayo, "Cults: In the Reign of Fire," *Time* (17 October 1994). Internet site: *http://www.rickross.com/reference/S_Groups5.html.*

14. Luc Jouret, "Transit pour le futur," trans. Ted Daniels, *Millennial Prophecy Report.* Internet site: *http://www.channel1.com/mpr/transit.html.*

15. Richard Lacayo, "Special Report: The Lure of the Cult," *Time* (7 April 1997). Internet site: *http://pathfinder.com/@@nJgHHgQAsL . . . m/970407/specia.the_lure_of_t.html.*

16. Jouret, "Transit pour le futur."

17. Ibid.

18. Ibid.

19. Barbara Demick, "48 Bodies Found in Swiss Villages," *Philadelphia Inquirer,* 6 October 1994, A1.

20. Ibid.

21. Lacayo, "Cults: In the Reign of Fire."

22. Ted Daniels, "Ordeal by Fire: The Tragedy of the Solar Temple," *Millennial Prophecy Report* 3, no. 6 (December 1994).

23. Ontario Consultants on Religious Tolerance, "Solar Temple (International Chivalric Order Solar Tradition)." Internet site: *http://www.religioustolerance.org/dc_solar.htm.*

24. Daniels, "Ordeal by Fire."

25. Lacayo, "Special Report."

26. According to the 11 October 1994, *Philadelphia Inquirer,* there were rumblings among members about alleged financial wrongdoing by Solar Temple members, as well as "Jouret's role in making and breaking marriages." Also, according to Ted Daniels's paper, "Ordeal by Fire: The Tragedy of the Solar Temple," "Rose-Marie Klaus, the disaffected wife of a member, held a press conference in which she condemned [the Order of the Solar Temple] for sex magic and the financial exploitation of its members." Internet site: *http://www.channel1.com/mpr/osthx.htm/.*

27. Ted Daniels, "The Life and Death of the Order of the Solar Temple," *Millennial Prophecy Report* 3, no. 5 (November 1994). Internet site: *http://www.channel1.com/mpr/ostbg.html.*

28. Daniels, "Ordeal by Fire."

29. Ibid.

30. Luc Jouret, "A tous ceux qui peuvent encore entendre la voix de la sagesse," trans. Ted Daniels, *Millennial Prophecy Report* 3, no. 5 (November 1994). Internet site: *http://www.channel1.com/mpr/vow.html.*

31. I am not suggesting that law enforcement did anything wrong with its prosecutions and investigations of Solar Temple, just as I am not saying that the U.S. ATF should not have investigated David Koresh's gun violations. No cult is above the law. They may react badly to an investigation, just as criminals will sometimes shoot at police when fleeing a crime scene, but it is not the fault of authorities when a group reacts in a harmful way. The issue should be: Is the group engaging in activities that are against the law and that could jeopardize the public welfare?

32. Michael Matza, "Mix of Apocalypse and Ego Drove Cultists with His Charm: Luc Jouret Built His Own World," *Philadelphia Inquirer,* 9 October 1994, A1.

33. Ibid.

34. Michael Serrill, "Remains of the Day," *Time,* (24 October 1994). Internet site: *http://www.rickross.com/reference/S_Groups6.html.*

35. Daniels, "Ordeal by Fire."

36. Lacayo, "Special Report."

37. Catherine Partsch, "Cults Spread Message of Fear," *Saint Petersburg* (Russia) *Press.* Internet site: *http://csde.aces,k12,ct.us.friends/spbweb/sppress/108/cults.html.*

38. "Deadly Cult Active in Petersburg," *St. Petersburg* (Russia) *Press.* Internet site: *http://csde.aces,k12,ct.us.friends/spbweb/sppress/111/deadly.html.*

39. David E. Kaplan and Andrew Marshall, *The Cult at the End of the World: The Incredible Story of Aum* (London: Random House, 1996), 291.

Chapter 6 Science Fiction Armageddon

1. Mervyn Rothstein, "Isaac Asimov, Whose Thoughts and Books Traveled the Universe, Is Dead at 72," *New York Times,* 7 April 1992. Internet site: *http://search.nytimes.com/books/97/03/23/lifetimes/asi-v-obit.html.* The other four *Foundation* books were *Foundation's Edge* (1982), *Foundation and Earth* (1986), *Prelude to Foundation* (1988), and *Forward the Foundation* (1993).

2. Kaplan and Marshall, *The Cult at the End of the World,* 12.

3. Ibid., 70.

4. Ibid., 67.

5. Ibid., 14.

6. Ibid., 7.

7. Ibid., 18.

8. Ibid., 48, 66.

9. Ibid., 17.

10. Ibid., 16.

11. Anthony Spaeth, "Engineer of Doom," *Time* (12 June 1995). Internet site: *http://pathfinder.com/@@kaMiQQQAqb . . . stic/1995/950612/950612.japan.html.*

12. Kaplan and Marshall, *The Cult at the End of the World,* 30.

13. Ibid., 31.

14. Ibid.

15. Ibid., 33.

16. These lawsuits forced the Cult Awareness Network (CAN) into bankruptcy. Scientology has since taken CAN's name and is trying to subvert CAN's original mission.

17. L. Ron Hubbard, *An Alien Affair* (Los Angeles: Bridge, 1985), 2.

18. L. Ron Hubbard, *Fortune of Fear* (Los Angeles: Bridge, 1986), from the cover.

19. From "Scientology," Spiritual Counterfeits Project fact sheet (Box 4308, Berkeley, CA 94704).

20. Richard Behar, "The Thriving Cult of Greed and Power," *Time* (6 May 1991): 51–53. By the way, the Church of Scientology filed a lawsuit against *Time* for publishing this article calling the group a cult of greed. In July 1996 a judge threw the case out, claiming that it wasn't defamatory.

21. Ralph Lee Smith, "Scientology—Menace to Mental Health," *Today's Health* (December 1968): 38. Cited by Walter Martin in *The Kingdom of the Cults*, rev. ed. (Minneapolis: Bethany, 1985), 346.

22. Behar, "The Thriving Cult," 51–53.

23. Kenneth Grant, *Outside the Circles of Time* (London: Frederick Muller, 1980), from jacket and page 50.

24. "Cult of the Month—Scientology: Pandora's Box," *Cornerstone* 31 (1976): 11,16, 23. Cited in Alnor, *UFOs in the New Age*, 194.

25. What one sees in today's Bible, simply put, is what has always been there. The discovery in 1948 of the Dead Sea Scrolls decisively proved that (among other existing proofs) no editing of the Bible ever took place. When the two-thousand-year-old scroll of the Book of Isaiah was compared to today's manuscripts, not a single change was discovered by experts!

Chapter 7 Flying Saucer Messiahs

1. From "The Message Given to Humanity by People from Space" found at the Raelian Movement's Internet site: *http://www.rael.org/English/e-pamphlet/e-pamphlet.html*. However, it is impossible to know at this time if these figures are correct. In 1992 the sect claimed thirty thousand members, but Susan Palmer's chapter "Women in the Raelian Movement," in *The Gods Have Landed*, ed. James R. Lewis (Albany: State University of New York Press, 1995), suggests that their membership figures are inflated.

2. Glenn Campbell, "Report of Rael Press Conference in Las Vegas, 3/11/97," *Area 51 Mailing List Archive*, at Internet site: *http://www.ufomind.com/area51/list.1997/mar/a12–002.shtml*.

3. Ibid. See also Palmer, "Women in the Raelian Movement," 107.

4. Ibid.

5. The Raelian Movement, "Help Us Welcome Extra-terrestrials," undated booklet. The Raelian claim about the swastika is at least partly true. It is an ancient occult symbol from India. Adolf Hitler took the symbol and slightly inverted it as the Nazi sign, intended to be the symbol of his one-thousand-year German kingdom—the Third Reich.

6. This is a typical tactic of cultic movements. For example, although Mormon leaders originally believed polygamy to be instituted by God for all time, it took the jailing of Mormon leaders by the U.S. government on polygamy charges to convince the church that it wasn't a good idea. Supposedly this came as a result of a "revelation" from God. But the fact is the supposed revelation came while Mormon leaders were in jail. The Mormon church has loosened up in other areas, as well, including the acceptance of

blacks into the higher levels of the priesthood. Vorilhon's change of symbols, however, appears to be more up front. He didn't claim a revelation before making the change.

7. Internet site: *http://rael.org.*

8. Palmer, "Women in the Raelian Movement," 106.

9. Ibid.

10. Alnor, *UFOs in the New Age,* 181.

11. Jacques Vallee, *Messengers of Deception* (Berkeley: And/Or Press, 1979), 144.

12. Internet site: *http://www.rael.org.*

13. Palmer, "Women in the Raelian Movement," 107.

14. Campbell, "Report of Rael Press Conference."

15. Claude Vorilhon, *Let's Welcome Our Fathers from Space: They Created Humanity in Their Laboratories* (Tokyo: AOM Corporation, 1986), 105.

16. Palmer, "Women in the Raelian Movement," 125.

17. Rael, *Let's Welcome Our Fathers from Space* (Tokyo: Raelian Foundation, 1987), 92, 95, 96.

18. According to Campbell, "Report of Rael Press Conference," conducted at the Flamingo Hotel in Las Vegas, Vorilhon claimed that Noah's ark in the Bible actually "flew above the seas."

19. Rael, *The Message Given to Me by Extra-terrestrials* (Tokyo: Raelian Foundation, 1986), 84.

20. Campbell, "Report of Rael Press Conference."

21. This Berkeley, California–based ministry has been on the front lines of giving Christian answers to the challenge of the cults since 1973.

22. Press release from the Raelian Movement, "Rael Creates the First Human Cloning Company," 10 March 1997. Internet site: *http://www.rael.org.*

23. Ibid. This quote is attributed directly to Vorilhon in the press release.

24. "Do not listen to those who try to frighten you by talking about the physical and especially the ethical after-effect which an abortion can cause," Vorilhon says. Cited by Palmer, "Women in the Raelian Movement," 112.

25. Ibid., 113.

26. Ibid. In fact Vorilhon separated from his own wife and children, according to Palmer. They have since joined his movement but are not reunited with him. Instead, Vorilhon travels in the company of several different women.

27. Ibid., 119.

28. Press release from the Raelian Movement, "UFO Land," 10 March 1997. Internet site: *http://www.rael.org.*

29. Palmer, "Women in the Raelian Movement," 111–12.

30. Ibid., 110.

31. Unarius Education Foundation, "A Resume of Unarius: Foreword to the Expectant New Student," undated.

32. Unarius Education Foundation, "That Rare, Unique, Treasured Commodity, Good News! Satan or the Anti-Christ Has Now Been Overcome!!" undated, 2. This statement is even more blasphemous when one considers that it equates the name *Jaweh* with Satan. Phonetically *Jaweh* and *Yaweh,* believed by Bible scholars to be the holy Hebrew name for God, are the same.

33. Curran, *In Advance of the Landing,* 33.

34. "Unarius Academy of Science—Mission Statement," undated. Internet site: *http:// www.serve.com/unarius/mission.html.*

189

35. This is only part of the Unarius 2001 prophecy that is found throughout its literature. See also Diana Tumminia and R. George Kirkpatrick, "Unarius," in *The Gods Have Landed*, ed. Lewis, 90; and "Unarius Academy of Science." Internet site: *http://www .teleport.com/~dkossy/unarius.html.*

36. Curran, *In Advance of the Landing*, 86. According to Tumminia and Kirkpatrick, "Unarius," at their first meeting Ernest Norman told Ruth that she had "once been the pharaoh's daughter who had found Moses in the bulrushes." See also "Cosmic Visionaries," an undated Unarius document at Internet site: *http://www.serve.com/unarius/ bio.html.*

37. Curran, *In Advance of the Landing*, 86.

38. Why then can't astronomers see the vast Martian civilization Ruth Norman claimed was there? Because it is underground!

39. This is remarkably similar to what happened during the waning days of the Heaven's Gate cult. Applewhite, claiming to be Jesus, was channeling revelations from God the Father, who he claimed was his departed spouse, Nettles! In the same vein, Unarians talk about the Normans as if they are still alive due to channeling. Ernest is now the Archangel Raphiel and Ruth is the Archangel Uriel.

40. Unarius Education Foundation, "A Resume of Unarius," 11.

41. "The Unarius Library" (El Cajon, Calif.: Unarius Education Foundation, undated catalogue), 23.

42. Ibid., 7.

43. Unarius Education Foundation, "A Resume of Unarius," 27–28. Note that this account contradicts the Bible in stating that Nicodemus purchased the corpse before he was dead. The Bible says that Roman soldiers made sure he died by thrusting a spear into his side and the Bible says quite clearly that Jesus died (John 19:34). Mary did not purchase the tomb, Joseph of Arimathea did (John 19:38). This account also fails to mention the Roman soldiers who were guarding the tomb, it denies the accounts of Jesus' meetings with people following the resurrection, and it denies his ascension into heaven (Acts 1:9–11).

44. "The Way of Thinking," undated. Internet site: *http://www.serve.com/unarius/ thinking.html.*

45. Tumminia and Kirkpatrick, "Unarius," 97–99. The cult may have more followers than these figures indicate, especially when considering that the group claims to have community access cable television stations nationwide and claims study groups in North Carolina; Ontario, Canada; and Nigeria.

46. Calder, *The Comet Is Coming*, 48.

47. Holy Tabernacle Ministries, "The Many Faces of Dr. Malachi Z. York." Internet site: *http://www2.gsu/edu/~phpgls/mzy.htm.* Perhaps needless to say, professional astronomers don't know where this planet and galaxy are; they are fictitious.

48. "Our Story!" Internet document explaining the history of the Holy Tabernacle Ministries. Internet site: *http://www.geocities.com/Area51/Corridor/4978/ourstory.html.*

49. Holy Tabernacle Ministries, "The Master Teacher Dr. Malachi Z. York." Internet site: *http://www.geocities.com/Area51/Corridor/4978/york.html.*

50. Holy Tabernacle Ministries, "The Many Faces of Dr. Malachi Z. York."

51. Malachi Z. York, "Debate One: I Am the Real Thing." Internet site: *http://www .netgenius.com/amom/debate1.htm.*

52. Holy Tabernacle Ministries, "The Many Faces of Dr. Malachi Z. York."

53. Malachi Z. York, "The God Concept," from *The Holy Tabernacle Family Guide.* Internet site: *http://www.netgenius.com/nuwaudu/god.htm.*

54. Holy Tabernacle Ministries, "The Master Teacher."

55. On a necklace beneath the feathers on the headdress is the cult's symbol: an Islamic crescent, a six-pointed star, and an ankh.

56. Malachi Z. York, "Extra-terrestrials and Creation," 83, 108–9. Internet site: *http://www.welch.jhu.edu/~dkmannee/scrolls.html.*

57. In my book *Soothsayers of the Second Advent,* 65–72, I looked at doomsday predictions of a similar phenomenon called the Jupiter Effect (or the parade of the planets) that occurred in 1982 that had *all* the planets lined up, which in theory was much greater than York's 2000 doomsday scenario. However, there was little effect from that alignment, which has occurred periodically throughout history.

58. York, "Extra-terrestrials and Creation," 83, 108–9.

59. "Order's Member Cited for Code Violations," *Macon* (Georgia) *Telegraph Online,* 24 April 1997. Internet site: *http://www.macontel.com/local/local424.htm.*

60. Malachi York, "Breaking the Spell!" Internet site: *http://www.geocities.com/Area51/Corridor/4978/spell.html.*

61. Malachi Z. York, "The Day of the Pentecost." Internet site: *http://www.welch.jhu.edu/~dkmannee/scrolls.html.*

62. Malachi Z. York, "Breaking the Spell." Internet site: *http://www.welch.jhu.edu/~dkmannee/scrolls.html.*

63. Holy Tabernacle Ministries, "The Master Teacher."

Chapter 8 Flying Saucer Deceivers

1. Randall Sullivan, "Aetherius Society: Sending Prayers to Jesus on Venus," *Los Angeles Herald Examiner,* 1 August 1983, B1.

2. These prayers do not resemble Christian prayers to God the Father. They are often repetitive mantras, like those used in Eastern mysticism and transcendental meditation. These prayers are shouted as the participants hold their palms to the machine.

3. Alnor, *UFOs in the New Age,* 90.

4. I personally do not give much credence to these reports after reading up on them, neither do NASA and most astronomers. First of all, the alleged face formation only shows up in detail on enhanced photographs that have gone through an *unorthodox* (and not generally recognized) enhancement procedure. Second, the alleged pyramids are not always there. They seem to blow away. Astronomers say such formations are not unusual for the planet, considering the tremendous cloudy wind gusts found there. In other words they are created by the wind on sand. The alleged city is pure speculation. Most scientists say these are mountainous structures, not the remains of buildings.

5. The Aetherius Society, "Sir George King: A Western Master of Yoga for the Aquarian Age." Internet site: *http://www.aetherius.org/bio.htm.*

6. The Aetherius Society, "The Aetherius Society: A Brief Introduction" (1989). Internet site: *http://www.aetherius.org/intro.htm.*

7. King claims the device, which sits atop a tripod, brings physical healing to people and can help stop future earth catastrophes, including earthquakes. He says that by holding one's hand to it while praying, the prayer power is stored in the device, which can be released by King later. He claims he has been able to store this power for future events. However, according to Douglas Curran, 69, King has been in poor health for years. The Bible teaches that God listens directly to our prayers and acts on them. No devices are needed.

8. The Aetherius Society, "Sir George King," 2.

9. The Aetherius Society, "Did the New Age Start on January 23rd, 1997?" Internet site: *http://www.aetherius.org/gaia.htm*.

10. Sullivan, "Aetherius Society," B6.

11. The Aetherius Society, "Operation Starlight: 19 Holy Mountains." Internet site: *http://www.aetherius.org/holymtns.htm*.

12. The Aetherius Society, "The Next Master Is Coming." Internet site: *http://www .aetherius.org/avatar.htm*.

13. Ibid.

14. Robert S. Ellwood Jr., *Words of the World's Religions* (Englewood Cliffs, N.J.: Prentice-Hall, 1977), 201–2.

15. Alnor, *UFOs in the New Age,* 186.

16. Walter Martin, "UFOs" (Rock Fellowship Church, Fresno, Calif., 14 June 1987).

17. This means in German the "Free Community of Interests for the Fringe and Spiritual Sciences and Ufological Studies."

18. For example, point 41 states: "Our teachings and views are directed toward reincarnation/rebirth in the sense of an evolution through the material life until the being becomes a pure spirit form and ultimately unifies with Creation itself." From FIGU, "What Is FIGU." Internet site: *http://web.eunet.ch:80/figu/FIGUHP51.HTM*.

19. Gary Kinder, *Light Years* (New York: Atlantic Monthly Press, 1987), from the jacket.

20. For example, Fred Bell, a popular UFO contactee, also claims extensive interaction with Semjase.

21. Dennis Stacy, "New Books," MUFON UFO *Journal* (February 1987): 11.

22. Kinder, *Light Years,* 224–25. According to an Internet page titled "Defamations and Intrigues" that was briefly on Meier's European Web site *(http://web.eunet. ch:80/FIGU),* Meier's organization in Switzerland, Meier and wife, Kalliope (Popi), have divorced, with her stating in court on 20 September 1996, that "I have never believed in this thing since it began." The page goes on to viciously denounce his ex-wife for her "slander and intrigues." The page complains about her announcing that Meier built UFO models of "wedding cake" and beamships from "lids of barrels between 1980 and 1982 to produce fraudulent photos with them." He denies this. "All of this is motivated by her endless hatred and vindictiveness for never being capable of taking my place and playing a leading role—something she always craved," Meier complains.

23. Kinder, *Light Years,* 218.

24. Kinder's book, *Light Years,* reports on this. Also the Mutual UFO Network released a 7 July 1987, letter from its Western States Director that states that "the other absolutely ridiculous claims of Meier relative to this incident are appalling! For instance, meeting God in space and photographing his eye!!!"

25. I did get into this case extensively on pages 165–75 in *UFOs in the New Age.*

26. Dawn Stover, "50 Years after Roswell," *Popular Science* (June 1997): 88.

27. Eduard "Billy" Meier, "My Youth," *Contact: Erra to Terra* (October 1989): 10.

28. Kinder, *Light Years,* 79.

29. Ibid., 84.

30. Ibid., 263.

31. Alnor, *UFOs in the New Age,* 171.

32. Ibid., 71.

33. Certain liberal scholars and those who call themselves "process theologians" would deny this doctrine. They state incorrectly that God is constantly changing; his attitudes and actions may not be the same today as they were in ancient times.

34. Internet site: *http://www.billymeier.com.*

35. Ibid.

36. See Alnor, *UFOs in the New Age,* 172–74.

37. The text on the Web page reads that Winters did these things "without ever having received any type of authorization to do so, without asking Billy for his permission or without compensating Billy in any manner." See Internet site: *http://web.eunet.ch:80/figu/FIGUHP67.HTM.*

38. "Lee Elders: A Cheat, Thief and Liar." Internet site: *http://web.eunet.ch:80/figu/FIGUHP67.HTM.*

Chapter 9 Visions of Ashtar

1. In recent years even Swiss contactee Billy Meier has claimed telepathic contact with Ashtar.

2. Don Ecker, "A Neo-Nazi ET? 'Hatonn's World'—Part II," *UFO* 7, no. 5 (1992): 8.

3. Don Ecker, "A Neo-Nazi ET? 'Hatonn's World'—Part I," *UFO* 7, no. 4 (1992): 30.

4. Ecker, "'Hatonn's World'—Part II," 9.

5. *UFO* magazine, P.O. Box 1053, Sunland, CA 91041, (818) 951-1250, ran a two-part exposé of the Hatonn/Ekker/Green controversy. Also see Internet site: *http://www.ufomagazine.com.*

6. Ruth Montgomery, author of a number of books dealing with UFOs, could be considered adept at automatic writing. She claims she goes into an altered state, sits down at her typewriter, and her fingers are guided, at lightning speed, to produce some of her occult literature. Two of the most famous trance channelers of this decade were Edgar Cayce, who used to dictate his revelations to his wife, with his eyes closed in the middle of the night, and Jane Roberts, who dictated the "Seth material" while in trances.

7. Ecker, "Hatonn's World—Part I," 30.

8. Paul Goodman, *History of the Jews,* ed. Israel Cohen (New York: E. P. Dutton, 1959), 182.

9. See "Channelings about Jesus' Ministry." Internet site: *http://www.pix.za/mbs/spirit/jesuschn.htm* and the FIGU Internet page that complains about Green. That's found at *http://web.eunet.ch:80/figu/FIGUHP65.HTM.*

10. Brownell, *UFOs: Key to Earth's Destiny!* 34–35, citing Van Tassel, *I Rode a Flying Saucer* (Los Angeles: New Age, 1952).

11. Curran, *In Advance of the Landing,* 81.

12. *Proceedings of the College of Universal Wisdom, Inc.* 8, no. 4, 4. *Proceedings* was the official publication of Van Tassel's organization. Among the items published in the magazine were the messages from the space brothers.

13. T. James, *Spacemen: Friends and Foes,* part 1 (Los Angeles: Understanding New Age Publishing, 1956), 2, 5. Cited in Alnor, *UFOs in the New Age,* 142.

14. James, *Spacemen,* 8, 11, 13, 17.

15. Ruth Norman, *Facts about UFOs* (El Cajon, Calif.: Unarius Education Foundation, 1982), 19.

16. Ashtar Command, *New World Order: Channeled Prophecies from Space,* ed. Carol Ann Rodriguez (1982; reprint, New Brunswick, N.J.: Inner Light, 1990).

17. Ashtar Command, *Project: World Evacuation,* comp. Tuella (Salt Lake City: Guardian Action International, 1982), from introduction.

18. Ashtar Command, *New World Order,* 5.

19. Ibid., 141.

20. "The Ashtar Command: Our Mission, Purpose and Directive." Spiritweb Internet site: *http://www.spiritweb.org/Spirit/our-mission-athena.html*. This message purports to be from Commander Lady Athena through Ashtar-Athena.

21. "Shan Chea Mother Ship Ready to Receive Guests," channeled through Tuella (Thelma Terrell) and found at *New Age On-Line Australia*. Internet site: *http://www.newage.com.au/ufo/mothership.html*.

22. "The Ashtar Command: Our Mission, Purpose and Directive," 2.

23. Not all groups claiming to be in touch with Ashtar or the Ashtar Command believe that only 144,000 people will be beamed aboard orbiting ships. Space does not permit me to delve into why so many UFO and New Age groups are taken with the number 144,000. But for further reading, chapter one of my book *UFOs in the New Age* is devoted to this issue. Apparently these groups are trying to draw an affinity with the Bible's Book of Revelation, chapters 7 and 14, which talks about the Messiah having 144,000 witnesses—Jews, 12,000 from each of the twelve tribes of Israel—who will remain pure during the tribulation, not rejecting Christ. By focusing in on this number without the biblical requirement that the 144,000 MUST be literal Jews is more evidence of an endtime delusion by those influenced by space-age mythology. It should also be noted that there are other cults, not associated with UFOs, that have also twisted these biblical passages, most notably the Jehovah's Witnesses, who claim that these witnesses come from their number!

24. For the best contemporary look at Sai Baba, see Tal Brooke, *Lord of the Air* (Eugene, Oreg.: Harvest House, 1990). Brooke, the president of the Spiritual Counterfeits Project of Berkeley, was at one time Sai Baba's top western disciple. He followed Baba to India, then was marvelously converted to Jesus Christ. For further information contact the Spiritual Counterfeits Project, P.O. Box 4308, Berkeley, CA 94704.

25. William Alnor, "The Christ Has Presented His Credentials to the Media, New Age Organization Says," *Christian Research Journal* (summer 1990): 35.

26. Ibid.

27. Rick Branch, "Is the Maitreya the Second Coming of Christ?" *Watchman Expositor* 8 (3 November 1991): 6.

28. Ibid.

29. Benjamin Creme, *The Reappearance of the Christ and the Masters of Wisdom* (Hollywood, Calif.: The Tara Center, 1980).

30. Ashtar, "Ascension, An Introduction," channeled by Eric Klein. Spiritweb Internet site: *http://www.spiritweb.org/Spirit/ascension-klein.html*.

31. Ibid., 5.

32. Ibid.

Chapter 10 A Litany of Lies and Other Deceptions

1. One of the deaths was that of a "copycat" suicide—a man not related to Heaven's Gate. The other was the 6 May 1997, death in a hotel room of a former Heaven's Gate member, who had entered into a suicide pact with another man, who survived.

2. This should not surprise us since the Bible says that spiritual things must be discerned spiritually (1 Cor. 2:14).

3. Dean Nelson, "To Heaven on a UFO?" *Christianity Today* (May 19, 1997): 14–15.

4. Clemens, "A Curious Pleasure Excursion," 246–47.

5. Clemens, "Extract from Captain Stormfield's Visit," 569–70.

6. Internet site: *http://www.newt.vallnet.com/~lora/heavensgate.html*.

7. The Hollywood film industry has helped create this mainstreaming effect. But it was also furthered by the growing acceptance of New Age channeling due to people like Shirley MacLaine (who claims her mission to sensitize the world to New Age occultism is being guided by aliens) and horror writer (and alleged contactee) Whitley Strieber.

8. Some writers have discussed the possibility that there may be a link between the Nephilim (giants) of Genesis 6 and a coming UFO delusion, a lie that will fool humankind on a massive scale just before the return of Christ. I believe this is a strong possibility. Some, like I. D. E. Thomas, Chuck Missler, and Mark Eastman, have put forward controversial views on this, giving credence to the stories of abducted women bearing half-alien babies that are raised by their demon-dads. The Bible tells us that the state of the world just prior to the coming of Christ will be "as it was in the days of Noah," and then judgment came (Luke 17:26–27). Could the Nephilim be returning as a UFO delusion?

9. John Keel, *UFOs: Operation Trojan Horse* (New York: G. P Putnam's Sons, 1970).

10. Vallee, *Messengers of Deception,* 21.

11. J. Allen Hynek and Jacques Vallee, *The Edge of Reality* (Chicago: Henry Regnery Company, 1975), xii–xiii.

12. Phil Cousineau, *UFOs: A Manual for the Millennium* (New York: HarperCollins, 1995), 151.

Appendix B Questions and Answers

1. John Ankerberg and John Weldon, *Facts on Astrology* (Eugene, Oreg.: Harvest House, 1988), 22.

2. Alnor, *UFOs in the New Age,* 41, 112.

3. Dave Hunt, "A Reason to Fear" (paper presented at Human Potential Foundation conference, Washington D.C., May 27–29, 1995); Alnor, *UFOs in the New Age,* 83.

4. Cited in Cousineau, *UFOs,* 179.

INDEX

William M. Alnor is president of Eastern Christian Outreach, Inc., in Philadelphia; publisher of *The Christian Sentinel* and the *EChO Extra;* and journalism instructor at Temple University. He also pastors Calvary Chapel of the Lehigh Valley. Web page addresses are *http://www.cclv.org* and *http://www.cultlink.com.*

Questions or comments concerning the subject matter of this book should be addressed to:

William M. Alnor
Eastern Christian Outreach
P.O. Box 133
Walnutport, PA 18088

Please enclose a self-addressed, stamped envelope.
Write if you would like to be on the mailing list to receive our ministry's publications, *The Christian Sentinel* and the *EChO Extra.*